D1741107

LUNDY
ROCK CLIMBS

by Robert Moulton

Maps and covers by Brian Wilkinson
Photodiagrams by Ken Wilson

PUBLISHED BY THE ROYAL NAVY AND ROYAL
MARINES MOUNTAINEERING CLUB WITH
FINANCIAL ASSISTANCE FROM THE BRITISH
MOUNTAINEERING COUNCIL

First Edition 1970
by R. D. Moulton

Second Edition 1974
by R. D. Moulton

Third Edition 1980
by R. D. Moulton

© Copyright R. D. Moulton
ISBN 0 904405 60 5

Cover illustrations:
Front Cover. The Devil's Chimney
drawing Brian Wilkinson
Back Cover. Stuart Bondi on Stingray
photograph Brian Wilkinson

Distributed by
CORDEE
249 Knighton Church Road, Leicester LE2 3JQ

Printed by Joseph Ward & Co. (Printers) Ltd, Dewsbury

CONTENTS

Acknowledgements

Firstly I would like to thank those climbers who have helped with this guide by providing comments on the climbing information: Pat Littlejohn, Frank Cannings, Charles Wand-Tetley, Brian Wilkinson, Tom McDonald, Roger Hughes, Arnis Strapcans, Andy Gallagher, Rowland Edwards and the many other climbers who have written to me over the years with comments on the climbs. Lundy's accessibility is such that all contributions such as these, both solicited and unsolicited, make a real input to the guide.

Inevitably this book owes much to its predecessors and my thanks are also due to those who helped with the previous editions: Admiral Keith Lawder, the late Peter Biven, Dave Brown, Keith Vickery, Pete Thexton, and again Pat Littlejohn and Frank Cannings.

Finally I would like to thank those who have contributed to the production of this book: Brian Wilkinson for the excellent maps, for both covers and for checking my typescript, Ken Wilson for the photodiagrams, Diane Moulton for checking my typescript, and the Royal Navy and Royal Marines Mountaineering Club, particularly Malcolm Rutherford and Bob Higgins, for making this book possible—the club's continued support in publishing regular guide books has done much to assist development of climbing on Lundy.

RDM 1980

Introduction

Lundy is a small island in the Bristol Channel which can only be reached by a two-hour crossing from the North Devon coast. This remoteness, combined with the rugged nature of the island and its sparse population, gives the climbing a strong atmosphere of isolation. The majority of the climbs are on sea level cliffs where the surroundings contribute greatly to the character of the climbing. The rock is granite, which varies in quality between the extremes of soundness and looseness. It need hardly be added that any accident on Lundy is likely to be considerably more serious than a similar accident on the mainland.

GENERAL

The island is leased by the Landmark Trust from the National Trust. Visitors, including climbers, are welcome but since there is only limited accommodation and camping facilities, it is important that all arrangements are made well in advance with The Agent, Lundy, via Ilfracombe, North Devon—telephone Barnstaple (0271) 73333. He will provide details of access permission, accommodation, sailings etc. There is between one and seven days delay, occasionally longer, in postal services to and from the island.

It is important that all climbers recognise the interests of others on the island, particularly bird watchers. While the relations between climbers and others on the island have to date been excellent, it should be appreciated that irresponsible or thoughtless behaviour by climbers could lead to severe restrictions being introduced.

The island is approached from Ilfracombe either by Motor Fishing Vessel (about two and a quarter hours) or by steamer (about one and a half hours). The latter only sails during the summer months, during which period there are generally sailings of one kind or another on Tuesdays, Thursdays, Saturdays and Sundays. In certain weather conditions, which occur relatively infrequently, it is impossible to land on Lundy—this can, of course, involve being stuck on the island for a day or more.

ACCOMMODATION
The following different types of accommodation are available:
—Millcombe House, the island's hotel.
—A number of cottages, for between 4 and 6 persons, which can be rented.
—The Old Light, a disused lighthouse with two detached buildings, which can accommodate up to 24.
—The Barn, a granite building which can accommodate 14.
—Camping, with a limit of no more than about 20 camping at any one time. It is essential to take a tent that can stand up to high winds.
In all cases, it is advisable to book well in advance or to be flexible in one's arrangements.

RESTRICTIONS ON CLIMBING DUE TO BIRD LIFE
Climbing is not allowed on certain cliffs during certain times of year, in particular from April to July inclusive. The restrictions vary from year to year and details are available from the Agent.

CLIMBING
The current state of climbing development on Lundy when combined with the island's inaccessibility is such that it has only been possible to make a limited check of the climbs described in this guide. A certain amount of inconsistency is to be expected both in the gradings and, to a lesser extent, in the descriptions.

MAPS
It should be possible to find all of the cliffs from the descriptions given in this guide. However, full 8 figure grid references are quoted for all the cliffs. The full 8 figures are for the most part academic and can only be used in conjunction with the Ordnance Survey 6 inch to the mile map of the island. The maps sold on the island are useful for exploration but they do not show the grid lines.

THE DESCRIPTIONS
Apart from the General Topography section, in which the main landmarks are described as one walks down the island, the cliffs are described in anti-clockwise order around the coast. Similarly on all cliffs the climbs are described from left to right. So that the user of this guide can automatically rely on these rules they have been followed rigorously even where a cliff is approached from the right hand side.

Descriptions of the whereabouts of the main areas and cliffs are given in the General Topography section. Subsequently the locations of the individual cliffs are described in more detail in the introductory notes to the area sections and sub-sections. The route descriptions are intended to be used in conjunction with these and with the introductory notes describing smaller sections of the cliff.

In all cases left and right are as the climber faces the cliff except for easy descents and where explicitly stated otherwise.

The general terrain on the descents and above many of the cliffs may be found potentially dangerous by climbers not used to similar undeveloped sea cliff areas. Other than indicating descents that are particularly harrowing (such as those to the Old Light Cliff and to Torrey Canyon) no specific warnings are given in the text.

Climbers, especially those visiting Lundy for the first time, are therefore advised to take particular care on such ground and not to take easy-looking terrain for granted. It is always a good idea to have a few spare ropes in a party visiting Lundy: not only for use in emergency but also because a fixed rope can often be useful for abseil descents, for a handrail on the steeper descents and for placement above a finishing stance on certain climbs.

The information given as to the accessibility of the starts of climbs is at best approximate since the difference between Spring and Neap Tides is considerable—certain low tide approaches are impossible at Neap Tides. Information as to tides can be gained from Tide Tables, local papers or from AA Books. High seas can make even the safest-looking approach to a sea level cliff dangerous.

Some indication has been given of the existence of the few pegs that are known to be in place. Such information should not be relied on too greatly and if in doubt pegs should be carried. As on all sea cliffs, pegs especially near sea level are liable to severe corrosion. Unnecessary pegs are not described.

There are a considerable number of small, generally broken cliffs and buttresses on Lundy that give climbs of up to 100 feet in length. In general such cliffs are only referred to in the general text and full route descriptions are omitted though in some cases the more significant lines are described in passing. Similarly there are a number of cliffs which give climbing of a go-anywhere nature on which disciplined route descriptions are superfluous.

GRADINGS

Adjectival or E gradings are given for all routes and numerical pitch grades are given for most of the pitches of 4a and above. In line with current practice, the number of sub-divisions below the Very Severe grade has been rationalised and in particular Very Difficult may now be found to be a somewhat tougher grade since it incorporates much of the ubiquitous Hard Very Difficult grade; likewise Hard Severe, which takes in many of the old Mild Very Severes.

It is assumed that climbers are conversant with E grades but for those who prefer the traditional Extreme grades, please read Mild Extremely Severe for E1, Extremely Severe for E2 and E3 and Hard Extremely Severe for E4.

The year of the first ascent is given in brackets after the adjectival grade and an asterisk indicates that there has been no known second ascent at the time of writing. This information can be used both as a cross-reference to the first ascents list and also to indicate the likely condition of a climb—for instance a (1970*) route may now be somewhat overgrown and any pegs left in place be corroded. The asterisks also gives an indication of gradings that are to be treated with some respect.

RECOMMENDED CLIMBS

The best climbing is on the west coast. In general, the east coast is best reserved for days on which strong west winds discourage climbing on the west coast although some of the climbs on the Knight Templar buttresses and on Gannet's Buttress are worth doing in their own right.

The following list of climbs is recommended as giving a selection of good climbs within each grade. This list is subjective and should not be taken too seriously—there are many other good climbs on the island, as can be seen from the route descriptions.

Moderate/Difficult:	Flying Buttress, Needle Rock, Seal Slab
Very Difficult:	Battery Rib, Flake Route, Walrus
Severe:	Devil's Slide, Quadratus Lumborum
Hard Severe:	Apsara, Devil's Spine, Eclipse, Shamrock
Very Severe:	Albion, Diamond Solitaire, Immaculate Slab, Ulysses Factor
Hard Very Severe:	Albacore, Formula One, Headline, Magic Flute, Overlord, Performance
E1:	American Beauty, Navigator
E2:	Magnificat, The Promised Land, Quatermass, Spacewalk
E3:	Antiworlds, Golden Gate, The Stone Tape

NOTE By coincidence rather than design the above list includes
all but two of the climbs in Pat Littlejohn's South-West
Climbs (Diadem 1979), the only two omissions being
Sambo and Stop Press. The only variation in grades
from those quoted in South-West Climbs is Magic Flute
and this was the result of wide consultation.

NEW ROUTES

Please send details of any new routes and corrections to this
guide to R. D. Moulton, 2 Gladstone Road, Buckhurst Hill,
Essex. In describing new routes and new cliffs please indicate the
location relative to any known features and routes and avoid
using cairns as reference points (these can be, and are, destroyed).
It is hoped to produce some form of new route supplement(s)
as and when necessary, and when circumstances permit.
Information as to what is available, even if only in note form,
can be obtained on request (stamped, self-addressed envelope
please) from R. D. Moulton at the above address.

Historical

The first climber known to have climbed on Lundy was Tom Longstaff in 1903 and 1927 when he climbed on St. James' Stone and on Gannet's Rock. However, the island's climbing potential was not realised until 1960 when Admiral Keith Lawder and Ted Pyatt visited the island on a day-trip and made a hurried round-tour to investigate the climbing possibilities. Suitably impressed they returned the following year with a stronger party. They crossed on the Lundy Gannet with Albion Harman (the then owner of Lundy) who, under the impression that this was the first climbing party to visit Lundy, ordered that rockets should be fired to mark their arrival. They concentrated their climbing on the most obvious features—the biggest of these and also the longest granite slab in Britain, the Devil's Slide, was climbed by Admiral Lawder and J. Logan. A trio of pinnacles was climbed: Needle Rock, the Devil's Chimney and the Constable—the latter two by Logan and Robin Shaw, who also found a way up Gannet's Buttress.

The records of climbing in the years up to 1965 are somewhat confused due to the loss of the Log Book in which details were being kept. The most notable new route during this period was Peter Biven and Vivian Stevenson's Albion, a worthy companion to the Devil's Slide and the most popular VS on the island. Otherwise, most of the development was on smaller cliffs in the Knight Templar Rock area and on the Flying Buttress. Among the lost records was the description of a route by Hugh Banner "somewhere in the Devil's Chimney area" that was said to be hard.

In 1965 a well-documented visit was made by a team from the Army Outward Bound School at Towyn. They concentrated on the Flying Buttress area, where in ignorance of any previous ascents they named and graded all the routes virtually from scratch. Some of the routes had undoubtedly been done before but the appearance of Diamond Solitaire was particularly worthy of note.

With one notable exception, the trend for the years 1966 to '69 was one of development of climbs at the easier grades. A lot of filling in was done in the Knight Templar Rock area, a number of small buttresses were developed and the Long Cliff was explored. On the last mentioned the Seal Slab routes are among the most pleasant of the easier climbs on the island. The one exception was a visit by a strong party from the University of

Bradford, a forerunner of the mass invasions of later years. They covered a lot of ground on the island and recorded new routes on seven different cliffs, the most significant of which was the impressive sea level cliff that they christened topically Torrey Canyon.

The publication of the first Lundy climbing guide in 1970 was followed almost immediately by important developments. South African climber Paul Fatti, while stormbound on the island, climbed a number of routes including the first lines on Focal Buttress and Fluted Face. Fatti also climbed Satan's Slip, an obvious challenge which claimed Lundy's first and so far only bolt. The other main activity of 1970 was during the first of a series of RNMC meets carried by a variety of modes of transport (on this occasion, a combination of DUKWs and a Tank Landing Craft) when Ian Howell and Peter Biven climbed two of Lundy's most impressive VSs on the same day, Ulysses Factor and The Kiln.

The first developments of 1971 were again during an RNMC meet (arriving this time by sea truck) when the South West's two strongest climbers, Frank Cannings and Pat Littlejohn, visited Lundy for the first time. Climbing separately, with Ken Wilson and Martin Chambers respectively, they each discovered their own new cliff and set to work on what were to be the first seriously gardened lines on the island—the justification for such tactics is obvious to anyone repeating the routes. Honours were divided about evenly: they provided Lundy with its first extremes in Magnificat and Juggernaut and also with two of its best Hard Very Severe's in Performance and Albacore, Soon afterwards, another strong West Country climber, Keith Darbyshire, made his first contribution with Shark. The year's final serious attempt at development ended in near disaster with Cannings' dramatic double rescue (the second was after the helicopter had ditched) after a bad fall on an easy (?) way down to Squires View Zawn. In the aftermath of the accident, Wilson teamed up with Pete Thexton to climb Seventh Seal and other members of the party climbed the first routes on the Fortress. The challenge of the Fortress was then taken up by Thexton with his excellent Valhalla, initially somewhat undergraded at Severe.

1972 was the year in which Littlejohn firmly established himself as the premier innovator on Lundy. Starting with a RNMC meet, which came by helicopter this time, during which Shamrock Corner was climbed (on St. Patrick's Day), the majority of the year's activity was in the Landing Craft Bay area. The most notable route was Littlejohn's Destiny but a feature of the area is the relatively large number of good routes of all standards. The year ended with the focus of attention elsewhere, in a significant two days during which the first lines were climbed on three of the biggest cliffs on the island: firstly, Graham Gilbert's Overlord on the Devil's Chimney Cliff and then Littlejohn's Wodwo on Weird Wall and Antiworlds in Deep Zawn.

The strongest party yet to have visited Lundy started the 1973 season off with a hectic week in which 33 new routes were climbed, probably the most active week of development in the history of British rock climbing. Littlejohn took possession of Deep Zawn, where he added a further five routes—The Stone Tape and Supernova being particularly impressive. The only other route in the zawn, Quatermass was contributed by Darbyshire who also found two routes on the cliffs between Sunset Promontory and the Old Light Cliff. Frank Cannings and John Kingston set to work with vigour in developing two relatively small cliffs, Bomber Buttress and Arch Zawn, on which they produced a grand total of 14 routes including Headline and Jetset. Graham Gilbert and Bob Moulton took over where Cannings had left off on Fluted Face and produced three further new routes, of which Magic Flute has become one of the most popular of the middle-grade routes on the island. They then moved north onto Squires View Cliff and the Fortress, where Good Vibrations on the former was the best of their routes. Inevitably the pace slackened somewhat after this onslaught but new routes continued to appear at a steady rate throughout 1973. Moby Dick on Alpine Buttress was a pointer to where future interest would lie but other activity was based on new small cliffs with climbs of all grades up to Hard VS. Pete Thexton was particularly active with routes such as The Green Light and The Vice.

A similar party, spearheaded by Littlejohn and Darbyshire, returned the following Easter and although the sheer quantity of new routes decreased to a mere eleven the previous year's quality was fully maintained if not surpassed. Littlejohn's and Darbyshire's best routes were The Promised Land and Spacewalk, both of which climb particularly dramatic areas of rock. They were joined on the latter by Thexton, who with Ken Wilson made worthwhile contributions in his own right—his best route being the excellent Wolfman Jack but Immaculate Slab was also very good at an easier standard. Later that year attention was focused on Montague Wall, which Darbyshire described as on first sight appearing to be heaving with semi-detached bungalows! Darbyshire made the first route on the Wall with Montague Python and this was followed by a further four new routes from a strong North Wales party including Ray

Evans and Cliff Phillips, who visited the island during indifferent weather in October.

Easter 1975 produced a mere handful of climbs partly due to the snow that was falling (a very rare event on Lundy) but equally to the much smaller party that was visiting. Pat Littlejohn and Dave Garner, however, found three good routes including Lundy's hardest slab climb in the superb American Beauty—a line that had been gardened the previous year by Thexton. Another worthwhile addition was Nick Allen's and Bob Moulton's Apsara, a dramatic Severe on Weird Wall.

Subsequent activity in 1976 centred on the relatively undeveloped line of cliffs between Sunset Promontory and the Old Light Cliff. Frank Cannings returned to the island with Bristol-based Arnis Strapcans and they climbed routes such as Eclipse, Sexcrime and Bleed for Speed. The biggest of their routes, however, was The Exorcist which takes a very steep blank wall in the Devil's Limekiln. Their interest in the Old Light area continued when they returned in 1977 and climbed Scorched Earth and Fusion among other routes. But again their most important route was in the Devil's Limekiln area with The Great Divide on Focal Buttress; this has been described by Littlejohn as "a unique jamming pitch—one of the purest in the country".

A strong party which combined the talents of Littlejohn, Cannings and Strapcans visited the island in August 1977. Littlejohn, after an absence of two and half years, produced a characteristic series of hard routes; most notable were those on Focal Buttress, Golden Gate and Olympica. During this visit Charles Wand-Tetley and R. Berry developed the pleasant and fairly amenable Black Bottom Buttress. Following Cannings' accident in 1971 the tradition of near-disasters on Lundy was maintained at the end of the year when during an otherwise unmemorable visit Les Holliwell was nearly washed out to sea by a 50-foot wave from the foot of Fluted Face and Bob Moulton set fire to his tent while attempting to change a gas cylinder.

The pace of development slackened in 1978 but a number of good routes were added by climbers from various parts of the country: Dark Power and Redspeed by the North Country climbers Roger Hughes and Leigh McGinley (Hughes had ventured into the Limekiln the previous year to unearth Flashing into the Dark), Genesis in Deep Zawn by Ken Wilkinson and George Hounson, and two new lines on the Albacore slab by Ken Lyle and R. Dean.

1979 started with three new routes from Devon climbers Brian Wilkinson and Andy Gallagher, the first "local" climbers to make their mark on Lundy since Littlejohn and Cannings. August and September of that year witnessed an upsurge of interest in climbing on the island with over twenty new routes being recorded. The most significant developments were in Grand Falls Zawn with Dennis Carr's A Separate Reality, and then Rowland Edwards' The China Syndrome and Grand Falls Road, the latter at 460 feet one of the longest climbs on Lundy. Other new climbs were generally much shorter in length but some good lines were climbed on rock previously ignored; another tendency was the continued exploration of the cliffs north of Long Ruse Ridge, where Bruce Goodwin's and John Vose's Out of the Blue was worthy of note.

General Topography of the Island

Good landmarks on the island are the three walls: the Quarter
Wall, the Halfway Wall and the Threequarter Wall. The top of the
island is in the form of a plateau 300 to 400 feet above sea level.
The cliffs between this and the sea are made up of grass slopes
and rock with the climbing cliffs being found at all heights above
the sea.

EAST COAST
Going north from the Landing Beach, the first climbing cliffs
encountered are the Quarries, between the Quarter and Halfway
Walls. Then follow the Halfway Buttresses at the east end of the
Halfway Wall. A few hundred yards north of the Halfway Wall
is the Knight Templar Rock. Some way north of the
Threequarter Wall and just past a curious depression running
into the sea, the Gannet's Combe, is the island of Gannet's Rock.
On the northern end of the island, some 300 yards south east of
the North Light and well above sea level is the pinnacle of the
Constable.

WEST COAST
On the south west tip of the island is the distinctive Great
Shutter Rock. Just inland from this is Focal Buttress and then
the Devil's Limekiln, a dramatic 300-foot hole. The bay
immediately north of Shutter Rock contains Weird and
Montague Walls and is bounded to the north by Montague
Buttress below the Montague Steps.

There are a number of sea cliffs between the Old Light and the
Quarter Wall—in particular, the Old Light Cliff immediately
below the Light, the Landing Craft Bay cliffs further north and
then, just south of the Quarter Wall and below the Old Battery,
the Flying Buttress.

The Halfway Wall ends in Jenny's Cove, which is bounded to the
south by Needle Rock. The Devil's Chimney, a 130-foot
pinnacle overshadowed by its mainland cliff, lies some 200 yards
up the coast. Immediately north of that is the very impressive
Deep Zawn. The curious rock formations of the Cheeses are
situated at plateau-level near the end of the Halfway Wall and
beneath these lie Egyptian Slabs. Further north the cliffs of
Jenny's Cove gradually loose height until the Cove terminates in
Beaufort Buttress.

The climbing in the bay north of Jenny's Cove lies firstly in Grand Falls Zawn and then on the cliffs either side of the large open zawn immediately beneath the Threequarter Wall.

The bay north of the Threequarter Wall is a major climbing area. At the south end of the bay is St. James' Stone. In the centre of the bay is the 400-foot slab of the Devil's Slide and to the north is Squire's View Zawn and the Fortress. The latter leads out to St. John's Stone, a smaller counterpart to St. James' Stone and the southern extremity of a shallow bay whose northern side is formed by the 250-yard Long Cliff. North of this is Arch Zawn and then a wide bay which terminates at the North West Point. At the south end of the bay are Long Ruse Ridge and Heron Zawn and in the centre is Cyclops Zawn.

East Coast

THE QUARRIES

Mostly these provide short pitches of up to 40-foot which, while not worth recording in detail, can give some climbing in sheltered surroundings.

From the Quarter Wall a track leads down to the Quarries. The first quarry encountered (OS Ref. 1376 4503) is distinguished by a goldfish pond at its foot. There is a simple short pegging pitch here.

The next quarry, the VC Quarry (OS Ref. 1386 4537), is some way further on. It provides a number of short climbs.

The quarry north of the VC Quarry (OS Ref. 1382 4559) gives some short climbs, including a 50-foot pegging pitch up the slightly impending wall on the left as one enters the quarry, above a dry stone wall. A more substantial climb is:

St. Loosifer   75 feet   E2   (1979*)
The easy-looking ramp in the left wall at the back of the quarry.
1 75 feet (5b). Climb the ramp, five peg runners (in place).

THE HALFWAY BUTTRESSES & KNIGHT TEMPLAR ROCK

The Halfway Buttresses are a group of six buttresses grouped around the east end of the Halfway Wall. Further north can be seen two much larger, rambling buttresses—these have come to be known as the First and Second Knight Templar respectively. The Knight Templar Rock itself is about 100 yards north of the Second Knight Templar.

The approaches to all these cliffs can be very tedious due to the prolific bracken in the autumn. At such times it is advisable to stay on the paths as much as possible, only venturing into the bracken when absolutely necessary.

THE HALFWAY BUTTRESSES   OS Ref. 1382 4590

The Halfway Wall ends in a pinnacle-buttress with the Logan Stone on its top. There is a climb, **Logan** (50 feet, Difficult), up the narrow seaward front of the buttress with short variation pitches up either side wall.

Below this buttress, in line with the Halfway Wall, is a larger buttress. This gives one climb, **Rubus** (90 feet, Severe), which takes the obvious line traversing diagonally left across the slab at the foot of the buttress and then continuing up blocks and corners to the top, avoiding the tenacious brambles as best as possible.

A few yards north of these two buttresses are three small buttresses. The left hand (southerly) and tallest buttress is very broken and heathery; it gives a couple of intermingled climbs (100 feet, Difficult) up its slabby seaward face. The central buttress is lower down and gives what is probably the best climb on the Halfway Buttresses, **Hard Labour** (60 feet, Very Severe) This goes up the left edge of the front of the buttress, up a crack to an overhang then up the continuation chimney above. The foot of the right hand buttress is separated from the summit of the central buttress by a small col; this buttress is small and gives an unpleasantly loose climb, **Blunderbuss** (40 feet, Very Difficult), up its seaward face.

There is one further buttress, higher up to the right; it is small and does not offer much scope except for boulder problems.

FIRST KNIGHT TEMPLAR   OS Ref. 1389 4603
The centre of the crag contains more vegetation than rock and the routes described are on either side. Twelve Bore takes the smooth white rib on the left and Bideford Ridge makes the best of the well defined but broken arête on the right.

Twelve Bore   90 feet   Severe   (1969)
A very enjoyable pitch. Start by scrambling up to a ledge 20-foot up below the smooth white rib.
1 90 feet. Climb directly up the rib for about 30 feet until above an overlap. Then move diagonally right and climb rounded cracks about 5 feet right of the arête to the top.

Bideford Ridge   110 feet   Difficult   (1963)
A rather broken and artificial line but the climbing is good. Start in a step in the arête about 40-foot up and below the first steep section.
1 30 feet. The block above is split by two cracks. Take the left hand crack or narrow chimney to a large ledge.
2 50 feet. Climb easily up the broken slab left of the arête for a few feet. Then traverse back right onto the arête above a short steep section and follow the arête to a ledge.
3 30 feet. Climb up to the left onto a flake and then up the short crack above to the top.

SECOND KNIGHT TEMPLAR   OS Ref. 1392 4607
The cliff is split by a large platform just above half height; the
ledge is more distinct to the right and more vegetated to the left.
Below the ledge in the centre of the cliff is a pink wall which is
broken and vegetated. The next climbs are on the steeper and
much cleaner rock right of this section.

Scafoid   165 feet   Very Severe   (1972)
The clean groove in the centre of the wall. Start below and to the
right of the groove.
1 95 feet (4c). Climb up to the groove and follow it, poor
protection, to the overhang. Move out right and up into a niche.
Climb the cracks above to a good ledge on Flake Route.
2 70 feet. Follow Flake Route to the top, up grooves.

Variation   **Foot Off**   95 feet   Very Severe   (1972)
1a 65 feet. Follow Scafoid to the overhang then traverse left to a
large sloping ledge, thread and peg belays.
2a 30 feet. Climb the chimney groove on the right to the ledge.

Flake Route   130 feet   Very Difficult   (1964)
Probably the best of the easier routes on the east side of the
island, quite an intimidating route for its standard. Start at the
bottom right hand corner of the smooth 50-foot wall below a
prominent jutting block.
1 20 feet. Climb easily over blocks to belay below a large flake
just right of the prominent block.
2 40 feet. Traverse steeply up to the left below the overhang
formed by the bottom of the flake. After 10 feet climb the
overhang on large holds to the crack up the left side of the
flake. Follow the crack to belay on top of the flake.
3 20 feet. Climb up to the ledge above and then up a short steep
groove to the halfway platform.
4 50 feet. Follow the obvious groove up the massive block to
the top.

KNIGHT TEMPLAR ROCK   OS Ref. 1387 4616
The central section of the south east side is capped by overhangs.
Heatwave takes the corner left of these and Crusader goes up to
the overhangs and then right to easier ground above the seaward
front of the buttress, which gives Saladin.

Heatwave   70 feet   Very Difficult
Start below the open groove in the left flank of the buttress.
1 35 feet. Climb up to a small overhang and pass this awkwardly
to the left. Move up and traverse left under an overhang to a
stance on a sloping ledge.
2 35 feet. Climb the steep groove immediately left of the
overhang to easier ground.

Variation Finish   40 feet   Very Severe
2a 40 feet. From the stance move back right and turn the
overhang on the right. Climb up for 15 feet and then move back
left awkwardly along a vegetated ledge to join the ordinary way.

Crusader   90 feet   Very Severe   (1963)
The second pitch though short is quite intimidating. Start below
the second groove to the left of the front of the buttress.
1 30 feet. Climb the groove until a slab with a good flake belay
is gained.
2 30 feet (4c). Climb up to the right of the narrow overhanging
chimney to a stance under the overhang.
3 30 feet. Traverse right across a slab to the nose and climb the
corner easily to the top.

Variation   **Direct Finish**   (1967)
A short steep problem.
2a 20 feet. Climb the wide shallow chimney right of the
overhangs and finish up the crack above.

A rather indefinite climb, **Sir Gareth** (90 feet, Severe), takes a
line up the broken, vegetated rock from the foot of Crusader to
the top of Saladin.

Big Ed   90 fee   Very Severe   (1978)
The rib 10 feet left of Saladin. Start below a small overhang
left of Saladin.
1 70 feet (4b). Turn the overhang on the right and make an
awkward step left onto the rib. Follow the rib over a bulge at
40 feet to the ledge in the front of the buttress.
2 20 feet. Finish as for Crusader or Saladin.

Saladin   90 feet   Very Severe   (1967)
A very good first pitch, sustained and steeper than it looks.
Start below the overlapping crack in the very front of the
buttress.

1 70 feet (4b). Climb the crack for 30 feet then follow the
obvious line up to the right until virtually on the arête. Continue
up to the large ledge on the left.
2 20 feet. Climb the easy corner above or the steep broken wall
on the right.

In the north (right hand) face there are two distinctive corners.
The first and more broken corner, which is very near the front
of the buttress, is:

Fag Ash   90 feet   Difficult   (1968)
Start below the corner.
1 50 feet. Climb broken rock to the foot of the corner proper.
2 40 feet. Climb the corner to the top.

White Horse   75 feet   Very Difficult   (1968)
Perhaps the best of the easier climbs on the cliff. Start beneath the
right hand corner.
1 35 feet. Climb up to the base of the chimney in the upper part
of the corner.
2 40 feet. Climb the chimney to the top.

GANNET'S ROCK AREA

Gannet's Buttress, the cliff that overlooks the Rock, is approached
by a steep path down the north flank of the buttress. This leads
to a ledge which breaks the buttress at half height. Scrambling
then leads down to the foot of the buttress. A few feet more of
scrambling lead down to the boulders that can be crossed at low
tide to reach Gannet's Rock.

GANNET'S BUTTRESS   OS Ref. 1365 4756

Below the halfway ledge the cliff is steep but very broken and it
is possible to climb virtually anywhere. This provides an
entertaining route, **Gannet's Traverse** (200 feet, Moderate), which
starts from the foot of the way down and takes a line diagonally
up to the left keeping below the halfway ledge until near the
left side of the buttress, where the cliff loses height and the
angle eases.

On the south face there is an extensive black wall above the
halfway ledge, which is reached by walking along the ledge or
by scrambling from the west side of the buttress. Near the left
end of the wall, about 100 feet left of the right-angled corner on
the right, is an inverted "U" overhang about 25 feet up—this
gives a short climb, **Gannex** (40 feet, Very Severe). Also starting
from the halfway ledge is:

The Squirmer 90 feet Very Severe (1967*)
Start below a break in the black wall with a jammed block,
about 25 feet left of the right-angled corner.
1 50 feet. Climb to the niche above the jammed block. Move
right along the sloping crack and then up to a higher crack. Go
right to a grass ledge and then up the crack above.
2 40 feet. Traverse left to a shallow cave. Climb the chimney
above and swing left across a slab to the finishing chimney.

The next two climbs start at the foot of the way down:

Gannet Front 225 feet Hard Very Severe (1961)
A fine climb taking the best line on the face; the hard moves on
the top pitch are in very exposed position. Start at the foot of
the easy way down at high water level.
1 100 feet. Take a line up easy rock to the left of the blunt arête
to a belay at the foot of a 25-foot groove.
2 25 feet (4b). Climb the groove and belay on the halfway ledge
below a large pinnacle.
3 100 feet (5a). Climb the pinnacle and then up a short shallow
groove. Move left and up to the bulging arête and cross this by
moving under a bulge to holds above an impending wall. Some
hard moves up the steep wall above lead to the finishing slabs.

Arrowhead 210 feet Very Severe (1966)
An impressive main pitch takes the overhung chimney in the
north eastern nose of the buttress above the halfway ledge. Start
as for Gannet Front.
1 100 feet. As for Gannet Front, climb easily to a belay below
the 25-foot groove.
2 50 feet (4a). Climb diagonally up to the left to the halfway
ledge. Walk back along the ledge and climb up broken rock to
the right of the pinnacle of Gannet Front then go right to belay
in a niche.
3 60 feet (4b). Climb steeply up into the chimney above using the
overhanging block above the belay. Follow the chimney and its
continuation to the top.

GANNET'S ROCK OS Ref. 1370 4758
The sea level boulders that lead out to the Rock can only be
crossed at, or fairly close to, low tide. The summit can be
reached by scrambling round to the south face and then by
taking a zig-zag line, with some Difficult standard climbing, to
the easy-angled seaward ridge. A route can also be made to the
seaward ridge across the north face, which is reached by
following the first 30 feet of Gannet's Rock Crack at Very
Difficult standard.

Gannet's Rock Crack   95 feet   Hard Severe
Start from a grass ledge with a prominent boulder about 30 feet immediately above the boulders between the Rock and the mainland.
1 45 feet. Climb a broken groove to the left to a ledge that leads round onto the north face. Climb up and back right to a belay ledge below the crack-line in the landward face.
2 50 feet. Follow the crack-line to the summit.

THE CONSTABLE   OS Ref. 1326 4802
This pinnacle rises out of a steep grassy slope, some 100 feet above the sea; it is almost 100 feet high on its seaward (north) face but only half that height on its inland face. The Constable is wedge-shaped with its narrow summit ridge running East to West. The Original Route takes a crack up the centre of the inland face.

Descent from the top of the Constable is by abseil and it may prove desirable to leave a longish sling.

Eveninawl   50 feet   Very Severe   (1971)
The left hand crack in the inland face, just left of the Original Route; strenuous but well protected. Start 20 feet left of the detached block of the Original Route.
1 50 feet (4b). Climb the corner to a difficult exit on the right. Traverse left and move awkwardly into an easy finishing crack.

The Original Route   40 feet   Hard Severe   (1961)
A strenuous but also quite technical pitch. Start on the inland (south) side by a detached block.
1 40 feet (4b). Climb up to the left to a steep crack, which is followed to a point six feet left of the summit.

Jude the Obscure   80 feet   Hard Very Severe (1979*)
A fine sustained pitch centred on the north east arête. Start at the foot of cracks in the east face.
1 80 feet (5a). Climb the cracks and swing onto the arête using a small flake. Stand on the flake and move right to a system of cracks on the north face and follow these to the top.

The Summons   80 feet   Hard Very Severe   (1971*)
An elegant pitch up the north west arête, both delicate and strenuous. Start at the foot of the arête proper.
1 80 feet (5a). Climb up broken rock on the right to a small sloping black ledge, which is gained by an awkward step from the right. Exposed climbing for 15 feet leads to good holds and then easier ground to the top.

West Coast—North of Threequarter Wall

The bay which contains the Devil's Slide is terminated by St. James' Stone to the South and by a similar, smaller counterpart to the North which has been named St. John's Stone. The north side of the small bay to the North of St. John's Stone is formed by a line of sea cliffs, about 250 yards long, between 100 feet and 200 feet high and cut by a number of small zawns. This line of cliffs, which face south, are referred to collectively as the Long Cliff; this contains the cliff Torrey Canyon at the south end and Seal Slab in its centre.

About 100 yards north of the Long Cliff is a large, steep-sided zawn which splits the headland at the south end of the large bay south of the North Light—this is Arch Zawn. About 150 yards north of Arch Zawn is Long Ruse Ridge; it should be noted that this is about 250 yards south of the "Long Ruse" or "Roost" that is marked on the 6″ and 5″ maps respectively.

There is a large bay south of the North Light. Heron Zawn splits the headland at the south end of the bay and Cyclops Zawn lies in the centre of the bay. The first climbing described lies above the north side of the bay.

ROCK POOL BUTTRESS   OS Ref. 1317 4787
About 400 yards south of the North Light is a group of small buttresses just below plateau level. Rock Pool Buttress is the third buttress going south from the North Light; it is due west of the point where the track starts to lose height and is distinguished (in most climatic conditions) by a rock pool on its flat summit. The approach to the foot of the buttress is by descending one of a number of grassy gullies between the buttresses.

Transition   120 feet   Very Difficult   (1969)
A line up the left flank of the buttress. Start below a subsidiary buttress left of the centre of the crag, just left of a triangular recess.
1 40 feet. Climb the broken groove left of the recess to a large ledge with a good belay.
2 60 feet. Climb a grassy crack line up slabs to the left to a stance on the north flank of the buttress, nut belay.
3 20 feet. Climb the wide, rounded cracks above to the top.

CYCLOPS ZAWN AND HERON ZAWN AREA
In the centre of the bay south of the North Light is a wide zawn with a boulder-strewn floor, Cyclops Zawn. South of this is a small zawn with Hidden Slab forming its north side. South again and some 150 yards north of Long Ruse Ridge is the larger, steep-walled Heron Zawn.

CYCLOPS ZAWN   OS Ref. 1305 4773
The name is taken from the distinctive buttress that rises from the back of the zawn and which has a large hole or "eye" near its summit (only visable from certain angles). North of this is a smooth south-facing slab which flanks a large west-facing wall overlooking the northern part of the zawn. The next climb lies on this wall.

Descent is by scrambling down to the north of the wall to gain the zawnbed boulders or, slightly harder, by scrambling down beneath the south-facing slab.

Out of the Blue   210 feet   Hard Very Severe   (1979*)
A fine route up a system of corners near the right edge of the wall and just left of the 10-foot basalt dyke. Start right of the dyke.
1 110 feet. Climb into a bay from the right and traverse left across the dyke. Follow a line into the slabby groove-line leading up to a pinnacle high up. Climb the groove and then slabs on the left to a peg (in place) and block belay.
2 50 feet. Traverse right, past two peg runners (in place), and move round the arête into a corner. Climb the corner to a ledge and peg belays.
3 50 feet. Finish up slabs to the left and scramble to large thread belays above.

HIDDEN SLAB   OS Ref. 1300 4770
The top of the slab is approached directly by scrambling down steep grass just south of the distinctive buttress rising from the back of Cyclops Zawn. Descent to sea level is by climbing down slightly to the north of the slab or by abseil down the slab itself.

The slab gives some pleasant 60-foot climbs of a go-anywhere nature, the most obvious and the easiest being the central crack which gives a Moderate climb. The wall on the north side of the way down gives two 50-foot Difficults.

GRAPEFRUIT BUTTRESS   OS Ref. 1304 4766
The buttress, which starts well above sea level, lies above and to he north of Heron Zawn.

Pomplemouse   80 feet   Hard Very Severe   (1979*)
Takes the main feature of the buttress, the large central corner
capped by a rounded overhang. A good strenuous pitch. Start at
the foot of the corner.
1 80 feet (5a). Climb the corner until a series of hard moves
allow a pancake on the right wall to be gained. Move up to the
overhang and climb this strenuously to the top.

HERON ZAWN   OS Ref. 1300 4765
Approach to Heron Zawn is by descending the grassy spur north
of the zawn to sea level and then traversing easily round into the
zawn at lowish tide. The only climbing to date lies on the slab
capped by a short wall in the north side of the entrance to the
zawn. All the climbs start on the platform formed by huge
blocks below the slab.

Rusty Silk   90 feet   E1 and A1   (1979*)
Start below the left side of the slab.
1 65 feet (5b and A1). Climb the slab to the horizontal break,
which leads to a good spike. Climb the overhang above with nuts
for aid. Belay above the overhang.
2 25 feet (4b). Move right into the groove of Slab and Groove,
and climb this for 10 feet. Step left and finish up cracks.

Salty Slip   100 feet   Very Severe   (1975)
Start by a block below the slab and left of the corner groove of
Slab and Groove.
1 100 feet. Climb up to the first horizontal break, traverse left
for 15 feet and then go diagonally left up to the second break.
Finish up the groove of Slab and Groove.

Channel Wrack   100 feet   Very Severe   (1979*)
A good climb with two contrasting pitches—there is still some
loose rock on the top pitch. Start as for Salty Slip.
1 60 feet. Climb the slab as for Salty Slip and continue straight
up to the second break then climb a thin crack. Traverse left to a
belay below an overhanging groove.
2 40 feet. Climb the crack right of the groove to a steep finish.

Slab and Groove   110 feet   Very Difficult   (1975)
Start below the corner at the back of the platform.
1 110 feet. Climb the corner to the second horizontal break in
the slab. Traverse left along the break to easy ground below a
conspicuous groove, which leads to the top.

LONG RUSE RIDGE   OS Ref. 1290 4750

The ridge is one of a number of ridges at the southern end of the large bay south of the North Light. It is the only long ridge in this area, all the other ridges being much shorter. The foot of the ridge is reached by scrambling down to its north; an approach from the south is also possible starting from the top of Arch Zawn.

Long Ruse Ridge   205 feet   Difficult   (1969)

A rather broken climb but with an attraction due to its isolated position. Start on a platform at the foot of the ridge, below a short steep wall.

1 35 feet. Climb up the broken line left of the wall then climb up to the right to a square ledge.

2 20 feet. Climb the steep groove above or steep broken rock on the right to a grassy col.

3 55 feet. Scramble up to the left then climb the steep broken left hand section of the wall above to the left side of the ridge. Continue easily round to the left to another grassy col.

4 25 feet. Move down to the right and climb a leftward-slanting crack in the slab above the col.

5 70 feet. Continue up the broken chimney to the top.

Variations

There are many variations on the basic theme and almost separate climbs of up to Severe standard can be made by linking together different pitches on the various blocks. The most substantial variations are at the bottom, where both the dyke right of the normal start and the flake right of that give good pitches. A good direct finish is given by the grey dyke above the small slab.

To the north of Arch Zawn is a 70-foot slab that provides some boulder problems: an easy crack rising from left to right, a harder line up the right edge and a thin line directly up the centre.

ARCH ZAWN   OS Ref. 1293 4738

This is the large steep-sided zawn 100 yards north of the Long Cliff. Various approaches to the top of the zawn are possible down grassy slopes.

Most of the climbing lies on the north side of the zawn. The west end of the cliffs on this side of the zawn is a small lichen-covered headland of excellent rock. The seaward face of this buttress gives two climbs which are approached by scrambling down to the north of the headland, initially down grassy slopes and then down broken rock. This is followed by a traverse back

south at sea level, crossing an inlet at lowish tide, to the foot of
the face. At higher tides, there is a higher exposed alternative
avoiding the inlet.

Margin 100 feet Very Severe (1973)
A pleasant climb taking a spectacular line over the overhang in
the left hand side of the seaward face. Start from the terrace
beneath the face.
1 100 feet (4c). Climb the slab to the overhang. Move left then
up to the large groove beneath the main overhang. Climb up to
reach a good handhold on the right, good nut runner, and swing
up to the right to clear the overhang. Continue up the crack
above to the top, peg belay or block belay well fack.

Frontispiece 150 feet Very Difficult (1973)
The very enjoyable first pitch takes the slab in the right hand
side of the seaward face; escape is then made up the obvious
ramp overlooking the zawn.
1 75 feet. Climb the groove then the slab to belay in the recess.
2 75 feet. Traverse easily right and go up the ramp for 15 feet.
Climb the groove on the left to the top.

Approach to the main zawn is by descending easy-angled grass
slopes on the south side of the zawn and then down easy rock
south of the zawn mouth to sea level platforms. A traverse is then
made back to the north at low to half tide to the boulders in the
zawnbed. An alternative approach can be made down the gully
at the back of the zawn with an initial 50-foot abseil.

The next two climbs are on the zawn wall of the headland. The
starting boulders are only accessible at low tide and not at all
at neap tides. A relatively short though dramatically undercut
abseil can be made from the ramp of Frontispiece to gain the
boulders when they are cut off.

Stop Press 145 feet E1 (1973*)
A fine climb up the left hand side of the main wall and then up a
crack in the exposed buttress above. Start from the left hand
pillar below the wall.
1 80 feet (5b). Step down to good holds, which lead up to a
traverse left to a large niche. Climb the diagonal crack on the
right to a block. Step left and climb the overhanging arête to a
smooth slab beneath an overhang. Use a peg for aid to step left
into a crack beneath the overhang, which is climbed on good
holds to a large recess on the top pitch of Frontispiece.
2 65 feet (5a). Climb straight up above the stance to a rising
traverse line. Climb this and then the crack on the right to the
top.

Headline 140 feet Hard Very Severe (1973)

A magnificent climb, which takes a spectacular line up the right hand side of the main wall. Start on the large blocks beneath the wall.

1 75 feet (5b). From the right hand block climb the wall directly to a bulge. Climb this strenuously moving up to the right then traverse right to a break in the overhangs. Climb through the break and traverse right for a further 15 feet to an exposed stance, nut belays.

2 65 feet (4c). Climb the open groove above the right end of the stance to the overhang. Move up to the left into another groove and climb the wide crack to the top.

Papa Joe 120 feet Severe (1973)

A pleasant climb, when dry, which goes up the corner crack and then the slab between the main buttress and the large slabs in the back of the zawn. Start beneath the crack at low tide.

1 120 feet. Climb the crack (good chockstone requiring a long sling) until it is possible to move right onto the slab. Climb the slab directly, crossing the top of a chimney, to the apex of the slab. Finish up ledges to a good thread belay.

Blizzard 140 feet Very Severe (1975*)

To the right of the crack and slab of Papa Joe are two ribs; the light grey right hand rib is conical in shape and leads to a short chimney. The route traverses right between two bands of overhangs and is pleasant with good situations. Start in the cleft left of the grey rib.

1 140 feet. Climb the cleft for a few feet and then pull strenuously right onto the rib. Go up a little then step across the rib and make a descending traverse right across slabs, almost to the lip of the lower overhangs. Climb straight up on good holds, over a rather suspect large flake, to a ledge (junction with Rainbow). Finish up easier rock as for Rainbow.

Rainbow 110 feet Very Severe (1973*)

A line up the centre of the large slabs to the left of the pinkish-coloured slab and corners of Purple People Eater. Start on top of the enormous boulder.

1 110 feet (4a). Step onto the slab and climb the overhang. Step right and then move up to the large crack on the right. Follow the corner left of the slab for 20 feet then traverse left on a band of large flakes until it is possible to break up to to the grassy slopes, peg belay.

Purple People Eater 150 feet E2 (1973*)
A serious undertaking, sustained and poorly protected. The most obvious feature in the right hand section of the north side of the zawn is a pinkish slab bounded on the left by corners. Start below the crack leading to an overhang to the left of the corners.
1 150 feet (5a). Climb the crack to the overhang and traverse right beneath it to gain the main groove. Follow this to another overhang then step right into the upper groove. Follow this and the corner above to the top.

Way Out 200 feet Hard Severe (1975*)
This takes a rather unpleasant but very distinctive black gully/ groove right of Purple People Eater and then trends left up the slabs right of that route. Start beneath the gully/groove.
1 100 feet. Climb the gully/groove direct on crumbly rock and either move left onto the slab at a slim short groove to a poor nut belay, or go higher up to a large spike on the right.
2 100 feet. From the stance at the base of the slabs, climb either of two broken crack lines straight up to finish over broken rock.

Footnote 210 feet Severe (1973)
Very loose in places, particularly on the top pitch. At the rear right hand (south) corner of the zawn is a large black slab. To the left of this is a subsidiary rib, the line of which continues as a slanting crack in the left hand wall of the slabs. Start beneath the rib.
1 100 feet. Climb the rib directly to a small pinnacle. Traverse left along the fault line to a small stance in a corner, peg belay.
2 110 feet. Follow the ramp up to the left and then traverse left along a grassy horizontal fault. After 15 feet follow the groove to the top.

The Arch that gives the zawn its name is a natural arch in the inland of two pinnacles or "rocks" at the south west corner of the zawn:

The Arch 70 feet Very Difficult (1973)
A pleasant little climb up an unusual feature. Start on the south side of the rock to the left of the arch.
1 70 feet. Climb a narrow slab up the seaward half of the rock to the summit. The easiest descent is down shelving slabs on the north west side of the seaward half of the arch, followed by a traverse right round the base of the arch and so back to the start.

There are two routes on the mainland cliff opposite and south of the Arch. Immediately opposite the gap of the Arch are two short grooves in the southerly-bounding arête of the zawn.

Arch Fiend   100 feet   Very Severe   (1973)
The right hand groove, a pleasant pitch with one move considerably harder than the rest of the climb.
1 100 feet (5a). Climb the groove, moving right at the top onto a large ledge. Make a hard move up the corner on the right and climb the crack above to the top, good spike belays.

The Flue   90 feet   Severe   (1973)
The obvious chimney in the corner to the right of the two short grooves.
1 60 feet (4b). Climb the chimney and exit left. Climb up to a belay on a large ledge on the right.
2 30 feet. Climb the continuation chimney and then the wall on its left to the top, huge block belays.

THE LONG CLIFF
The slope above the Long Cliff is made up of steep grass and a number of small lichen-covered buttresses. Numerous descents to the top of the sea cliffs can be made down the steep grass. It is also possible to traverse along the top of the cliffs from either side. A good landmark is Crenellation Buttress, the tallest of the lichen-covered buttresses at about 100-foot; it is directly above Seal Slab and is distinguished by its summit which is shaped like a battlement. Seal Slab itself faces north and is in the centre of the Long Cliff. To the left of Seal Slab is a deep zawn capped by a conspicuous overhang which can be seen as far down the West Coast as Jenny's Cove.

SHORT STORY ZAWN   OS Ref. 1288 4728
The Long Cliff ends to the north in the small Short Story zawn about 100 yards south of Arch Zawn and just north of a small headland. The climbs in the zawn are approached by scrambling down the broken rock that bounds the zawn to the north.

Big Shiner   100 feet   Hard Severe   (1970)
The obvious overhanging crack in the north (left) side of the zawn. Start beneath the crack and directly opposite the black basalt vein of Short Story.
1 100 feet (4a). Climb the crack, which slants slightly left, to the top.

Jug of Punch   130 feet   Hard Severe   (1974)
An enjoyable and impressive pitch, which climbs the steep slab
in the back of the zawn, 30 feet right of Big Shiner. Start next to a
large boulder below a blunt rib.
1 130 feet. Climb the rib for 20 feet and move awkwardly onto
the slab. Climb up to the right to an exposed ledge and continue
steeply back left under the large overhang. Climb the groove
above until an obvious hand-traverse left can be made to a good
ledge and the top.

Short Story   120 feet   Severe   (1969)
The central slanting fault line in the south side of the zawn.
Start by crossing the zawn to a platform below a narrow slab
slanting towards the mainland.
1 90 feet. Climb up to the large crack in the slab and follow this
tending left at the top.
2 30 feet. Move right with difficulty to gain a ledge by way of
the basalt dyke. Move up from the left end of the ledge on
suspect holds for a few feet to finish.

PHANTOM ZAWN   OS Ref. 1291 4723
60 yards south of Short Story Zawn and just north of Seal Slab
is Phantom Zawn, which is distinguished by two caves in its
interior.

Dark Power   150 feet   E3   (1978*)
A cunning diagonal line to join the base of the obvious right
hand of the twin cracks in the impending south wall of the zawn.
Very steep climbing with excellent rock and protection. The
approach is by diagonal abseil down the seaward face to a tidal
ledge at the foot of the south arête of the zawn.
1 80 feet (5b). Climb twin cracks on the left to a large overhang.
Turn this on the left and gain a cracked groove, which is followed
to its end. Exit left into a niche, nut belay.
2 70 feet (5c). Climb the left arête of the niche to a standing
position on a line of grey flakes. After placing protection,
swing down and hand-traverse the grey flakes with difficulty
until a crack is gained after 15 feet. Climb the strenuous crack
to the top.

SEAL SLAB AREA   OS Ref. 1295 4718
The next climb (OS Ref. 1292 4720) is approached by
descending the blunt arête that bounds that small zawn north of
Seal Slab to the north. The descent is by a short climb, **Carpenter**
(60 feet, Very Difficult), which goes down the arête to a platform
just above sea level—the main difficulty being provided by a
short corner.

Alice   230 feet   Severe   (1968)
A long traversing climb on which only the first pitch is harder than Very Difficult. Start at low tide on the sea level platform.
1 40 feet. Move left along a ledge and start up the corner as for Carpenter. Part way up the corner move left onto the steep wall and cross it on small holds to reach a steep shallow gully.
2 50 feet. Descend the gully to a 3-foot ledge just above the sea. Follow the ledge to the left to belay at a higher level.
3 80 feet. Climb the nose left of a deep recess then go left onto good holds, which are followed to the foot of twin cracks.
4 60 feet. Climb the left hand crack to a broad earthy ledge. Finish up the small tower above.

Variation Finish   75 feet   Severe
4a 75 feet. Take the obvious rising traverse line leftwards for about 35 feet. Climb a corner and then a shallow chimney to the top.

The approach to Seal Slab itself is by descending the shallow gully south of the top of the slab. Where the gully fades out continue down steep broken rock trending right (facing out) to ledges at the foot of the 200-foot slab.

Seal Slab gives very enjoyable climbing in impressive surroundings. It is possible to climb virtually anywhere up the slab. However, two basically independent lines are described—both are well worth while.

Walrus   200 feet   Very Difficult   (1967)
Pegs may be useful for belays although a reasonable selection of nuts should suffice. Start at the left end of the ledge at the foot of the slab. Climb up a groove line and move up right onto the main slab. Climb diagonally up to the left and step onto a nose above an overhang. Continue up steep grey crystalline rock and then on up lichen-covered rock to the top.

Seal Slab   180 feet   Difficult   (1966)
Start below the right edge of the slab. Climb leftwards and follow a line more or less up the centre of the slab. Numerous lines are possible in the upper section.

CRENELLATION BUTTRESS

Crenellation Groove   90 feet   Severe   (1966)
A rather slight pitch taking the open and lightly vegetated groove in the nose of the buttress. Start right of the foot of the buttress.
1 90 feet (4a). Climb up left to the foot of the groove and follow it to the top.

TORREY CANYON   OS Ref. 1304 4716
This is the steep cliff at the right end of the Long Cliff. Approach
to the foot of the cliff is by a steep descent down the valley/
zawn south of the cliff. The first 20 feet down the southerly side
of the head of the valley are particularly earthy and unstable,
thus making this one of the more desperate descents on the
island, but easier ground is soon reached (fixed rope useful).

The crag is characterised by a central gully which is almost a
small zawn.

Norseman   140 feet   Very Severe   (1967)
A fine route up the bulging left hand corner crack of the central
gully. Start on the sloping ledge below the left arête.
1 110 feet (4b). Climb up blocks to the right to gain the corner.
Climb the bulging corner to a large ledge on the left, peg belay.
2 30 feet. Climb a wide crack to the top.

Rehabilitation Wall   150 feet   Difficult   (1967)
This climbs the west-facing slab that forms the right side of the
central gully. It can be climbed by a number of lines.

Cornflake Crack   140 feet   Very Severe   (1967)
A serious, poorly protected route with crumbly rock in its upper
section. The climb takes the prominent flake crack a few feet to
the right of the arête right of Rehabilitation Wall. Start below
the crack.
1 140 feet (4c). Scramble up to the foot of the crack proper.
Climb the crack and its narrow continuation chimney to the top.

In the right hand end of the crag is a prominent pod-shaped
crack with a clean cut corner immediately to its left. These give
the lines of Conger and Stingray respectively.

Stingray   110 feet   Hard Very Severe   (1967)
A fine climb. Start at the foot of the corner.
1 80 feet (4c). Climb the corner to a small stance on top of the
huge flake that forms the left wall of the corner.
2 30 feet (4c). Climb the loose continuation of the corner, moving
right at the top.

Conger   100 feet   Hard Very Severe   (1974*)
A worthy companion to Stingray. Strenuous climbing up the
pod-shaped crack is followed by an exposed finish. Start below
the crack.
1 100 feet (4c). Climb up into the crack and follow it, moving
right at the top. Climb the arête to the top.

CHRISTOS BITAS BUTTRESS   OS Ref. 1307 4712
This is the cliff just south of Torrey Canyon on the opposite side
of the open zawn. The approach is as for Torrey Canyon.

The crest of the buttress running down from the top of the cliff,
first as a narrow ridge and then as a steep arête, divides the cliff.
To the north is a lichenous face above a triangular pinnacle and
to the south the cliff is dominated by two main grooves slanting
from right to left.

Demian   200 feet   Very Severe   (1979*)
The left hand groove, a good main pitch. Start below the groove.
1 80 feet (4c). Climb the groove to the overhang, step left onto
the steep slab and climb the narrow continuation ramp with
difficulty, peg runner (not in place), to a small ledge. Nut belays.
2 120 feet (4b). Traverse diagonally right to the stance on Reprise
and continue right along a ramp. Go back left and traverse right
to a crack and flakes, which lead to the top.

Reprise   190 feet   Hard Very Severe   (1979*)
The steeper and higher, right hand groove is followed by a pitch
up the crest of the buttress. A good route with a fine crucial
pitch on excellent rock. Start beneath the groove.
1 80 feet (5a). Climb the groove pleasantly to a ledge. Climb the
groove above with difficulty to a small ledge and nut belay just
left of the arête.
2 110 feet (4b). Follow steep and exposed cracks on the crest of
the buttress to a ledge. Easier climbing in the same line leads to
the top—care with the rock needed.

THE FORTRESS   OS Ref. 1309 4703
This is the steep south-facing sea cliff, about 150 feet high, on
the mainland spur leading out to St. John's Stone. The western
aspect of the cliff is a steep turret-like nose that overlooks St.
John's Stone; to the right of this the face is seamed with
vertical crack lines. A wide bouldery ledge cuts across the face at
half height and continues round to the back of the cliff.

The approach is from the inland side of the face by a steep wide
grassy ramp leading down to the halfway ledge from the grassy
col known as Squires View. The ledge can also be approached
by scrambling round the back (north) of the cliff.

The next two climbs lie on the seaward nose of the cliff. The
starts are approached by scrambling from the halfway ledge down
the blunt south western rib of the buttress, just right
(facing out) of a narrow gully, to a ledge some 25 feet above
high tide level.

Blood Axe   145 feet   Hard Very Severe   (1971*)
A steep climb up the actual nose of the Fortress.
1 70 feet (4a). Traverse left and slightly down on good flakes to
a steep crack leading up from the sea. Climb the crack, passing
a small bulge, to the halfway ledge.
2 75 feet (5b). Immediately above is a steep leftward-trending
groove, some 15 feet right of the edge of the face and right of
a narrow crack. Climb the groove using a nut for aid and move
left awkwardly to a peculiar projection. Move up and step left
onto a small knob, from which some difficult moves lead to the
top. Scrambling leads off to the right.

Siegfried   135 feet   Hard Severe   (1971)
A rather slight climb up the right hand edge of the nose, moving
right in its upper sections until near the slim groove of Prospero.
1 60 feet. Move right from the ledge and cross the narrow gully
to gain the obvious rounded rib, which is followed to a stance at
the narrowest point of the halfway ledge.
2 75 feet (4a). Climb the flat-topped pinnacle immediately above
the stance. Move right into the base of a steep crack then
traverse out right for 10 feet until good holds lead steeply to an
exposed rib and a ledge belay. Scrambling leads to the top.

Prospero   165 feet   Hard Very Severe   (1973*)
A very sustained climb which finishes with interesting climbing
up the left hand of the long grooves in the left hand section of
the south face. Approach is by abseil as for Valhalla. Start at
low tide on the sea level ledges below the fifth crack to the left
of the corner of Valhalla—this crack is the last one before a 15
feet wide smooth wall, some 40 feet left of Valhalla.
1 65 feet (5a). Climb the steep crack to the halfway ledge and
belay beneath the deep groove left of the undercut section of the
upper wall.
2 100 feet (5a). Climb the groove all the way to the top.

Valhalla   140 feet   Very Severe   (1971)
A very good main pitch, varied and sustained, which takes the
long groove right of the overhangs in the south face of the
Fortress. Start by abseilling to ledges at the foot of the large
corner in the centre of the lower wall of the south face.
1 40 feet. Climb the corner to the halfway ledge.
2 100 feet (4b). Climb a short wall to gain the groove above and
follow it to the top.

Hel   90 feet   Hard Very Severe   (1971)
The groove to the right of Valhalla. Start on the halfway ledge
below the central groove some 10 feet right of Valhalla.
1 90 feet (5a). Climb the groove to the top with a difficult move
at about half height, some 15 feet below a ledge.

SQUIRES VIEW ZAWN

The zawn/inlet north of the Devil's Slide splits into three shallow
valleys at its head. On the north side of the northerly of these
valleys is a domed lichen-covered buttress facing south. This is
split by three chimneys, each of which gives an 80-foot to 100-
foot climb at Difficult to Very Difficult standard.

The foot of the zawn is characterised by a huge diamond-shaped
wall, the top half of which is lichen-covered. To the right (west)
of this wall is a 120-foot pinnacle. This is Forgotten Pinnacle,
whose claim to being a pinnacle is somewhat tenuous since only
its top 10 feet or so are separated from the mainland cliff.

The dammed stream immediately north of the Devil's Slide, which
flows down the southerly of the three valleys, can be followed
down to a steep grass slope leading down an open gully leftwards
(facing out) beneath the foot of the diamond-shaped wall—fixed
rope useful. This way down though steep and demanding care is
recommended in preference to other more immediately obvious
descents.

SQUIRES VIEW CLIFF   OS Ref. 1317 4702

This is on the north side of the zawn, opposite Forgotten Pinnacle.
The climbs described are all on the right hand end of the wall,
where the rock has a somewhat gritty texture and is not always
above suspicion but some of the climbing is very good. The most
prominent feature is the very clean cut groove of The Stray in
the upper part of the wall near its right edge. Belays at the top
of the cliff can be quite hard to find; a good belay, which can be
used for all the routes, is provided by a block just to the left of
the top of The Stray—the alternative is a peg belay well back.

Good Vibrations   170 feet   E1   (1973)
A fine sustained main pitch takes a diagonal line up the steep
slab immediately left of The Stray—some loose rock. Start to
the left of the slab below a basalt dyke slanting slightly left.
1 60 feet (4a). Climb the line of the dyke for 40 feet, passing a
bulge, then climb a short slab on the right to a stance below the
main slab, peg and nut belays.

2 110 feet (5a). Climb the corner above for 20 feet then make a rising traverse across the steep slab on the right below a small overlap, which is climbed after 10 feet. Continue in this general line to a point some 10 feet above the big overhang where a crack is joined. Follow the crack and then the arête to the top.

Bloody Ages   125 feet   Very Severe   (1973*)
A direct line up the cliff crossing the diagonal line of Good Vibrations. Start as for The Stray, some 30 feet left of the foot of the groove of that climb and below a short steep corner.
1 50 feet (4b). Climb the short corner and continue on suspicious rock trending slightly left to the stance on Good Vibrations below the slab of that climb, peg and nut belays.
2 75 feet (4c). Climb the corner above to a grassy ledge below a steep section. Move up to the right and round into a wide chimney, which is followed to the top and an exit left to finish.

The Stray   160 feet   Very Severe   (1972)
A fine line with a good first pitch though the top pitch is slightly marred by poor rock near the top. Start some 30 feet to the left of the foot of the obvious groove, below a short steep corner.
1 90 feet (4b). Climb the corner then follow a rightward-trending corner forming the left edge of a slab and climb up to the foot of the groove. Nut belay at the base of the groove, avoiding a moving block.
2 70 feet (4c). Climb the groove to the top.

Digitalis   150 feet   Hard Very Severe   (1973*)
The arête right of The Stray, which is approached from the big groove on the right. Start left of the foot of the groove.
1 60 feet (5b). Climb a rightward-slanting rake, easily at first, until a hard move, peg runner, leads into the foot of the big groove. Climb the groove to a nut, peg and spike belay below the overhang on the left.
2 35 feet (5a). Climb up to the left using the crack below the overhang to the arête. Pull onto the arête and climb a groove, past a rocking stone, to a constricted stance with nut and flake belays just right of the groove of The Stray.
3 55 feet (4b). Climb the cracks in the left side of the arête to the top.

Breakaway   155 feet   Hard Very Severe   (1973*)
This takes the big groove on the right—the first pitch is in
common with Digitalis. Start as for that climb.
1 60 feet (5b). Climb a rightward-slanting rake, easily at first,
until a hard move, peg runner, leads into the foot of the big
groove. Climb the groove to a nut, peg and spike belay below the
overhang on the left.
2 50 feet (5a). Climb the corner on the right then the slab
trending right to a ledge, poor peg belay.
3 45 feet. Step left and climb the loose dyke to the top.

ST. PETER'S STONE   OS Ref. 1312 4698
This is the large square high-tide island in Squire's View Zawn.
It provides a very good view point for the surrounding cliffs.

St. Peter's Stone   70 feet   Very Difficult   (1971)
Start at low tide below the leftward-slanting crack in the landward
face of the island.
1 25 feet. Climb the crack to a stance.
2 45 feet. Continue up the corner above then move left to broken
rock and thence to the top. Descent is by abseiling or by climbing
down the same route.

FORGOTTEN PINNACLE   OS Ref. 1314 4695

Forget-me-not   120 feet   Very Severe   (1970*)
A greasy repulsive climb of some character up the corner left of
Forgotten Pinnacle, between it and the diamond-shaped wall.
1 35 feet. Climb the corner to a flake stance on the right.
2 60 feet (4b). Continue up the corner, now a narrow chimney,
to a recess.
3 25 feet. Climb broken rock to the summit of Forgotten
Pinnacle and then easily across to the mainland.

Forgotten Pinnacle   120 feet   Hard Severe   (1967)
A good climb up the easy-angled groove running up the left
side of the pinnacle. Start below the groove.
1 40 feet. Climb up to the ledges at the foot of the groove.
2 80 feet (4b). Climb the groove to the point where it ends at a
shoulder. The obvious way from here is to step left to easy ground
but it is better to step up right into a crack, which is climbed to
the summit. Climb easily across to the mainland.

Echo   140 feet   Very Severe   (1974*)
The obvious slanting parallel cracks in the seaward face of the
pinnacle. Start below the cracks.
1 140 feet. Climb easily up to the cracks and follow them,
avoiding a few loose blocks just below the top.

DEVIL'S SLIDE AREA

The cliffs that form the back (north) of the Devil's Slide are divided into two sections by a steep gully. To the left is Fluted Face, 250 feet high and split by a sloping terrace at half height—below the terrace is a steep white wall and above a lichen-covered face with a number of obvious gardened lines. To the left (north) of Fluted Face the cliffs lose height and a grassy spur goes down almost to sea level; further north again is an indeterminate 80-foot cliff and then Forgotten Pinnacle.

Between Fluted Face and the Devil's Slide is first the steep gully and then a number of lichen-covered walls and ribs above a steep yellow and black wall.

The climbs at the back of the Slide start from a large area of ledges below the gully right of Fluted Face. The most interesting though somewhat lengthy, approach is by means of Dexter (see page 45). When this approach is impossible due to tides, the sea or just inclination, the ledges can be reached by a 70-foot abseil from the left hand (facing out) end of the terrace that crosses Fluted Face. The terrace is approached by descending one of the grassy gullies immediately north of the summit of the Slide to the grass slopes to the north (right facing out) of Fluted Face.

FLUTED FACE   OS Ref. 1314 4692

The upper face provides a number of excellent sustained pitches at a steep slab angle with small holds. Apart from on Tempest, the climbing actually on the lower face tends to be more broken but the position, directly above the sea, and the rock are both very good. Apart from Magnificat any combination of pitches above and below the terrace can be used, the most appropriate borrowings being the first pitch of Performance for Magic Flute and the first pitch of Tempest for Performance.

The best starting stance for the four climbs actually on the face is on nuts in a small groove in the left hand bounding arête of the area of ledges, some 20 feet below the overhangs above.

Tempest   250 feet   E1   (1973)
The most substantial of the four routes on the face, having an excellent first pitch and some very precarious climbing near the top.
1 110 feet (5a). Climb easily up the arête and traverse 15 feet left to the crack as for Performance, nut runner. Step down and traverse left for a further 10 feet to a thin crack line, which is climbed more or less directly to the halfway terrace.
2 90 feet (4b). Climb the twin cracks in the left side of the wall. Continue up the narrow continuation groove until it is possible

to move left to an obvious spike. Move left and climb a shallow groove forming the left side of a large flake. Stance on top of the flake, poor peg belay in situ.

3 50 feet (5b/c). Traverse back right from the flake for 10 feet into the main crack line. Climb delicately up this with a move out right after 10 feet onto a rounded ledge, then go back into the crack and on to a ledge. Nut belay above the next ledge. Scrambling to the top.

Performance   230 feet   Hard Very Severe   (1971)
A very good climb whose sustained main pitch takes the left hand of the long grooves in the right section of the face above the terrace. A large selection of medium to large nuts is required for protection.

1 90 feet (4b). Climb easily up the arête then traverse left fot 15 feet into a crack line, which is climbed to the terrace. Spike belay beneath a short square-cut crack.

2 140 feet (5a). Climb the crack for 10 feet then the continuation twin cracks to a small ledge below a long groove. Take the crack on the left until it peters out then move back right into the main groove. Continue directly up this and when the angle eases traverse right to a stance on the easy rib, spike and nut belays. Scrambling to the top.

Magic Flute   200 feet   Hard Very Severe   (1973)
A very enjoyable climb and the least affected by vegetation, the easiest of the Fluted Face climbs. The main pitch takes the central and deepest groove in the upper wall. Although close to its neighbours it is quite independent.

1 70 feet (4a). Climb easily up the arête to the overhang. Move left and climb steeply up on large holds for a few moves. Instead of moving easily right below the bulge above, go over the bulge and climb rounded cracks to the halfway terrace.

2 130 feet (4c). Climb the short square-cut crack as for Performance. After 10 feet move out right on rounded flakes and climb cracks to the foot of the central groove. Climb the groove to its top, exiting right to the easy rib, nut and flake belays. Scrambling to the top.

Sandpiper   190 feet   Hard Very Severe   (1973)
Another good route whose main pitch takes the right hand groove immediately left of the slender rib of Magnificat.

1 70 feet. Climb easily up the arête to the overhang and move left onto the slab. Climb steeply up on good holds then go easily back right into a groove, which is followed to the terrace.

2 120 feet (5a). Climb the steep twin cracks some 15 feet right of the short square-cut crack of Performance. Move slightly right into the right hand groove, which is followed to a stance on the easy rib above, nut and flake belay. Scrambling to the top.

Magnificat   175 feet   E2   (1971)

A hard, technically interesting route which finishes up the narrow rib forming the right edge of Fluted Face. Start on the sea level ledges beneath a prominent groove threading its way between a series of small overhangs to the left of the steep gully.

1 75 feet (5a). Climb up to the groove making a difficult move to gain its foot. Continue up the groove and turn the overhang to the left. Climb either of the grooves above to a stance.

2 50 feet (4a). Move into the crack above the stance then step left onto the arête and follow this via a crack to a pinnacle stance and peg belay.

3 50 feet (5b/c). Climb the rib above with increasing difficulty to a stance and spike belays. Scrambling to the top.

THE BACK OF THE SLIDE

The lowest section of the face right of Fluted Face is a steep slab rising out of the sea—Dexter traverses across this slab. Above the slab and below the upper lichen-covered face is an impending yellow/black-streaked wall split by the clean groove of Redspeed. Seventh Seal starts up the gully on the left (the steep gully right of Fluted Face) and then traverses right above the impending wall to climb the central rib in the lichen-covered face. The rounded right hand rib of the face is Devil's Spine.

Seventh Seal   185 feet   Hard Very Severe   (1971)

After steep climbing up the gully, some impressive situations are encountered in the centre of the face on the right—now fairly loose in parts of its upper pitches. Start below the steep chimney/groove forming the lower part of the gully.

1 45 feet (4c). Climb the groove until a difficult move leads to a good jug. Stance and peg belay above.

2 30 feet (4a). Traverse easily right under a large flake and gain its top by a crack. Belay lower down right of the flake.

3 60 feet (4c). Step right to a steep crack and follow this until it is possible to gain a ledge on the right. Climb up leftwards more easily then follow a series of ledges up the rib to a stance.

4 50 feet. Climb the rib above then move right onto the rib of Devil's Spine, which leads via a short crack on the right to a block belay. Scrambling to the top.

Redspeed   130 feet   E1   (1978*)
An enjoyable route which takes the groove in the middle of the
buttress between Fluted Face and the Slide. Start at the right
hand side of the ledges below the central gully.
1 130 feet (5b). Follow the line of flakes towards the large
overhangs. Traverse right for a few feet to gain a narrow
slanting ramp. Climb this then move back left to reach the foot of
the main groove. Climb the groove to its top, spike belay.
Finish up Devil's Spine or, more appropriately, traverse right
and climb Shark.

Variation
The main groove can also be reached by going up to the roof,
which is passed by a difficult move rightwards—harder.

THE DEVIL'S SLIDE   OS Ref. 1314 4688
This is the smooth slab, 400 feet high and 75 to 50 feet wide. At
the foot of the slab is a prominent large smooth block, which is
sea-washed at high tide. To approach the block, scramble down
the grassy gully south (left facing out) of the Slide then move
left (facing out) to climb down the narrow rib south of the Slide
at a Moderate standard. At high tide the climbs can be started
from a horizontal crack crossing the slab 25 feet up.

The next three climbs are in fact on the back of the Slide but are
approached via the foot of the Slide by walking/scrambling as
far as possible to the north to a large block belay, some 20 yards
left of the Slide proper.

Dexter   90 feet   Hard Severe   (1970)
A pleasant low to half tide approach to Fluted Face.
1 90 feet (4b). Move left onto the slabby face and climb down a
crack to the left for 15 feet. Continue along the obvious traverse
to the left, moving down below a bulge, to the large area of
ledges.

Devil's Honeymoon   125 feet   Very Severe   (1976)
A rather slight route but with some good climbing on pitch 1 up
the left flank of the Devil's Spine.
1 65 feet (4c). Move left and climb a leftward-trending groove
to the overlap, which is taken direct to a small stance and nut
belay.
2 60 feet (4b). Traverse left for a few feet then climb diagonally
leftwards to a corner, which is climbed to a good stance adjacent
to Devil's Spine. Finish as for that route.

Devil's Spine   215 feet   Hard Severe   (1963/1973)
A very pleasant climb, quite sustained for its standard and
harder when wet, which takes the prominent rib 50 to 25 feet
left of the Slide. Protection is sparse but with nuts adequate.
1 80 feet (4b). Go up to the left then steeply back right to climb
the rounded rib above. Nut and poor flake belay on a small
ledge.
2 40 feet (4a). Climb the centre of the lichenous depression to a
ledge with a block belay at the point where the rib develops into
a well-defined arête.
3 70 feet (4a). Climb the arête. Where its steepens climb its left
side back to a notch in the arête. Continue up the next steep
step in the arête to another notch and a flake belay.
4 25 feet. Traverse right for a few feet and climb a short groove
back to the arête and a block belay. Scrambling to the top.

Devil Dodger   225 feet   Hard Severe   (1970)
A poor climb which starts up the broken rib bounding the Slide
on the left and the takes the gully on the left. Start below the
broken rib.
1 90 feet. Climb steep broken rock to gain the left edge of the
Slide. Continue up this to a belay.
2 110 feet (4a). Continue up the broken rib until it steepens then
move left into the gully and climb this. Where the gully steepens
climb diagonally left to belay on the prominent flakes on the
arête of Devil's Spine. A poorly protected pitch with some
vegetation. This pitch can be made easier and a bit pointless by
traversing onto Devil's Spine lower down.
3 25 feet. Move right for a few feet then follow a short groove
back onto the arête as for Devil's Spine. Scrambling to the top.

Shark   200 feet   Hard Very Severe   (1971)
A magnificently positioned pitch with some bold moves at its
top up the elegant rock fin overlooking the top section of the
Slide. Start by traversing across the crack line crossing the
Slide at half height to a stance on the left edge.
1 130 feet (5a). Climb the groove in the steep arête to a peg
runner. Climb the smooth slab to the overhang, which is turned
on the right to gain a deep crack. Belay on the flat-topped block.
2 70 feet. Climb blocks to the top.

The following climbs are on the Slide proper, whose upper half
provides a number of fine sustained slab pitches in magnificent
position. The lower half of the Slide is at a slightly easier angle
and can be climbed anywhere at a Difficult to Very Difficult
standard—a feature that is shared by Devil Dodger and avoided

by Shark. In this respect the lower sections of all the climbs are
formalities; however, these pitches provide pleasant approaches
to the upper sections of the Slide and they add something to the
atmosphere of climbing on the Slide.

Albion 350 feet Very Severe (1963)
The third pitch up the black corner bounding the Slide to the
left gives excellent sustained climbing and is one of the best
pitches on the island—the remaining pitches are much easier.
Start below the left edge of the Slide.
1 120 feet. Climb easily up the left hand side of the slab then
traverse left to a stance on the bounding rib.
2 80 feet. Move back right and climb the slab to a small stance
with flake belays beneath the impressive retaining wall on the
left.
3 120 feet (4c). Climb the curving corner above and continue
more easily to a stance and block belay beneath the headwall.
The pitch can be shortened by belaying in the corner on nuts
and a small flake.
4 30 feet. Climb up to the left as for the Devil's Slide.

Variation **Direct Finish** 25 feet Hard Very Severe (1971)
4a 25 feet. Climb the crack in the headwall with two pegs for aid.

Satan's Slip 360 feet Hard Very Severe (1970)
A direct line up the centre of the Slide. The main pitch is not
technically hard—nowhere is it really thin—but it is very
sustained and poorly protected. The bolt runner is now in a very
poor state but since small wires can be placed its replacement
would seem unnecessary. Start below the centre of the Slide.
1 25 feet. Climb easily to a stance on the horizontal crack.
2 125 feet. Climb the centre of the Slide to an awkward nut or
peg belay to the right on the halfway fault line.
3 140 feet (4c). Trend to the left and climb up just right of the
black streaks and just left of some overlaps to a bolt runner (in
situ) at 90 feet. Continue over an overlap to the point where the
black streaks meet the corner of Albion. Climb the corner for
10 feet to belay on a small flake.
4 70 feet (4a). Move into the centre of the Slide and climb up
left of the lightly-vegetated groove to the traverse of the Devil's
Slide route, which leads to the left to finish.

The Devil's Slide   390 feet   Severe   (1961)   *5/9/83   J.T.E.*
The classic route of the island. The lower pitches are easy but
above these the climbing gradually increases in difficulty until
the airy final traverse. Pegs should be carried for the higher
belays. Start on the large block at the foot of the Slide.
1 70 feet. Climb easily up the right side of the Slide.
2 100 feet. Continue in the same line to the halfway fault line.
Either use a peg belay or traverse right to belay on the large
flake in the grassy gully. If a 120-foot rope is being used it is
worth belaying on a peg a few feet higher.
3 130 feet. Take an indefinite line up the right hand bounding
rib of the Slide, to the right of a white scoop, or climb the
scoop itself—harder. Peg belays on ledges—if a long enough
rope is being used it may be preferable to continue some way up
the next pitch in search of good peg cracks.
4 90 feet. Climb up the right edge of the Slide until level with
the point where it steepens into a headwall. Traverse left along
the obvious line, with increasing difficulty, then climb blocks on
the left to the top.

Variations
The traverse at the top can be avoided by climbing off the Slide
to the right—easier and less worthwhile.

Direct Finish   70 feet   Very Severe   (1971)
4a 70 feet (4c). Climb the edge of the Slide as for the normal
route. Instead of the traverse left climb straight up to a bulging
groove, which is climbed to the top—quite delicate.

DEVIL'S SLIDE APPROACH CLIFF   OS Ref. 1315 4684
When seen from the foot of the Slide there is the slender rib of
the way down immediately right of the Slide. Right of this rib is a
100-foot cliff of excellent rock; unfortunately the cliff is very
broken and it is possible to climb virtually anywhere.

Just right of the slender rib are a series of corners and ribs, which
give some pleasant 50-foot pitches. By combining one of these
with the obvious smooth groove on the right in the lichen-
covered rock above an enjoyable if artificial climb can be made,
Gollum (100 feet, Very Difficult).

Further round to the right the south side of the cliff also gives
some climbing, though the lines are not so obvious.

ST. JAMES' STONE AREA

The next route lies on a small sea level buttress (OS Ref. 1315 4678) due south of a rock island—this is just west of the main zawn immediately north of St. James' Stone. The ledges at the foot of the buttress are approached by abseil.

Starship Trooper   110 feet   E2   (1979*)
The open V-groove in the left hand side of the buttress, a good bridging pitch. Start on a small sea level ledge or on a small stance above high water level.
1 110 feet (5b). Climb the groove to the top, peg runners at 40 and 80 feet (in place).

An escape route from the ledges below the buttress, **Klingon** (110 feet, Very Difficult), can be made by following cracks up the arête of the buttress right of the previous route.

ST. JAMES' STONE   OS Ref. 1304 4675

This rocky promontory is gained by walking over the neck of land connecting it to the mainland.

In fact there are two Stones: an Inner Stone and an Outer Stone. It is quite an interesting scramble over the Inner Stone to get to he Outer Stone. Further scrambling leads down to the sea at various points of the Outer Stone.

There is a considerable amount of good and enjoyable climbing at Difficult to Very Difficult standard up the many obvious lines on all sides of both the Inner and the Outer Stones. Much of the climbing involves descents, traverses and then ascents. The nature of the rock is such that the climber is best left to discover his own lines.

West Coast—Central Section

THREEQUARTER WALL AREA

Immediately west of the Threequarter Wall is a deep zawn
reaching back almost to the end of the wall. The northern edge of
the zawn is formed by a rounded easy-angle sea-level buttress,
whose southern counterpart is the Parthenos. North of the easy-
angled buttress the grass slopes above end in two open gullies of
overhanging grass which are divided by a narrow rib. The next
two climbs are on the next buttress to the north (OS Ref. 1313
4659), which is immediately south of a similar buttress that has
to its north a distinctive 10-foot wide zawn.

Descent is by grass to the top of the buttress, passing beneath
the steep plateau-level Black Bottom Buttress. Continue down
grass on the south flank of the sea-level buttress and then
scramble down Moderate standard rock, passing a narrow ledge
leading across to the arête of the buttress (the stance above the
first pitches of both climbs), to a ledge just above high tide level.

Quadratus Lumborum   150 feet   Severe   (1971)   9/9/83 → T.E. MD
                                                                    A.T
A pleasant and increasingly popular climb in good situation which
follows the arête of the buttress. Start at the north end of the
ledge, below a slab.
1 40 feet. Climb the thin crack a few feet right of the arête (as
for Talcum). After 25 feet, make a difficult move left to gain the
arête and continue up this to the narrow ledge, nut belay
2 70 feet. Follow the obvious traverse across the left wall of the
buttress, descending initially and then ascending, to a steep wall,
which is climbed by a zig zag line to a good ledge and belays.
3 40 feet. Climb the wall above to finish.

Talcum   70 feet   Very Difficult   (1971)
Start on the ledge and below the slab.
1 40 feet. Climb the thin crack a few feet right of the arête then
take an obvious line to the right to another thin crack, which
leads to the narrow ledge. Nut belys.
2 30 feet. Climb the twin cracks on the right.

BLACK BOTTOM BUTTRESS   OS Ref. 1322 4663
This is the plateau-level buttress immediately north of the
Threequarter Wall. The rock is excellent and the protection good.

Conga Corner   105 feet   Very Severe   (1977)
The leftward-slanting crack line in the left side of the buttress.
A good sustained pitch.
1 65 feet (4c). Climb the crack, moving left at the hanging flake,
and then the continuation chimney. Belay left of the top of the
chimney.
2 40 feet. Follow a series of ramps to the top.

Funky Chicken   90 feet   Very Severe   (1977*)
Start at the foot of the slanting crack as for Conga Corner.
1 90 feet (4b). Climb the crack of Conga Corner to the hanging
flake then climb the flake and step right. Climb the groove and
the crack above to the top.

Pancake Shuffle   105 feet   Hard Very Severe   (1977)
An exciting climb. Start beneath the overhang in the right side
of the buttress.
1 45 feet (5b). Climb the steep slab to the short corner right of
the overhang then make a hard traverse left, past the pancake,
and climb into the twin cracks in the front face of the buttress.
2 60 feet (4c). Continue up the cracks then move straight up to
a bold finish.

THE PARTHENOS   OS Ref. 1317 4649
This sea cliff lies in the centre of the cove north of Jenny's Cove
and south of St. James' Stone. The crag is about 100 yards
south of the Threequarter Wall and is directly opposite the large
rock island of St. Mark's Stone.

The main face is very steep indeed with a huge hanging corner
on the left and large black overhangs in the centre. The two
routes described are on the right hand side.

The top of the cliff is reached by scrambling down steep grassy
slopes. The foot of the cliff is then reached by climbing down
steep broken rock south of the crag (left facing out)—a traverse
is then made back north at sea level.

Dyke   120 feet   Very Severe   (1967)
A good climb up the obvious dyke running up through slabs and
overhangs. Start 50 feet right of the main face, below the dyke.
1 120 feet (4c). Follow the line of the dyke in its entirety, with a
difficult overhang at 80 feet and hard finish.

Start   80 feet   Severe   (1967*)
The obvious line right of the basalt dyke taken by the previous climb. Start about halfway between the basalt dyke and the way down.
1 80 feet. Climb up onto the slab, which is climbed by a crack to gain a small niche just right of a sentry-box. Climb the niche direct and finish up a shallow corner. Peg belay.

GRAND FALLS ZAWN   OS Ref. 1320 4641

To the north of Beaufort Buttress and south of the Parthenos are two large zawns. The first, Double Headed Zawn, is deeply incut and pronounced while the second is much shallower with a very tall slab (taken by American Beauty) forming its back wall.

Approach to the foot of the zawn is by descending the ridge just north of the zawn (as for the Parthenos—rope useful) and then traversing south at one of a number of levels depending on the state of the sea—Difficult standard climbing. The traverse leads to the foot of a large pillar leaning against the cliff at the edge of the inner zawn—depending on the level of the traverse the pillar may be hard to recognise as such. Approach to the zawnbed boulders beyond the pillar (to start A Separate Reality and American Beauty) is only possible for two hours either side of low tide. The main pitches of the former route can, however, be approached either by following the high tide approach for Grand Falls Road or by climbing the easy groove left of the pillar.

The left hand wall of the zawn looks loose but gives climbing on relatively sound rock. Above and to the right of the pillar is a large scoop whose base is formed by a smooth brown slab. A Separate Reality takes the right hand side of the scoop whereas The China Syndrome takes a diagonal line up from the left to climb the left side of the scoop.

The China Syndrome   330 feet   Hard Very Severe   (1979*)
A fine climb, mainly on good rock and with impressive top pitches. After starting up a crack left of the pillar the climb takes a long diagonal line up to the right to finish near the highest part of the cliff. Start left of the pillar and below a crack system leading up to the right of a small square overhang.
1 50 feet (4b). Climb the cracks and belay on the left edge of the buttress below the overhang.
2 150 feet (4b). Climb the cracks on the right until it is possible to move rightwards along a ledge system (various belays possible), which leads to a belay on the arête overlooking the inner zawn.
3 60 feet (4b). Step down and traverse right along an earthy ledge into a crack system leading up to the top of the large

scoop. Follow the lower crack until it is possible to move up into the higher crack. Follow this for ten feet to a belay.
4 70 feet (4c/5a). Follow the crack-line for a few feet then traverse right across a steep slab into the middle of the face. Climb a groove to a pinnacle and move back left into the crack. Climb up and across cracks to get into the bottom of the V-groove. Finish either up the groove and exit left, or continue up the steep crack—harder.

Gorgeous Guano   170 feet   Very Severe   (1979*)
A direct line above the pillar which crosses the previous route near the top of the cliff. Start below the two big grooves in the seaward face of the pillar.
1 75 feet. Climb the left hand groove and belay on top of the pillar.
2 100 feet. Climb a groove on the left then move right and up to easier ground. Climb over a large flake on the left and traverse left to a spike (The China Syndrome crosses here). Finish up the left edge of the slab above.

A Separate Reality   250 feet   E1   (1979*)
An excellent climb with a very impressive top pitch in fine position and good protection. Start in the inner zawn, opposite the slab of American Beauty and below a chockstone-filled groove just left of square-cut overhangs.
1 75 feet (4c). Climb the groove to a peg and nut belay below the top of the pillar.
2 85 feet (5a). Traverse right to a spike. Climb the rightward-slanting crack for a few feet then go up a groove and follow a line of holds up to the right until it is possible to step up onto the large slab. Climb up to a peg belay in the centre of the slab . Or continue up the rightward-slanting crack and move right before gaining the slab—harder.
3 90 feet (5a/b). Follow the weakness in the slab diagonally up to the right until the overlap can be climbed. Move up and left on good holds until a hard move is made into the groove formed by the obvious overhanging nose. Climb the groove to the top. Belay well back.

Grand Falls Road   460 feet   Hard Very Severe   (1979)
A tremendous route of great character with impressive situations and on good rock. It takes a diagonal line, almost a girdle traverse, up the wall overlooking the American Beauty slab. Start on flat ledges at the foot of the pillar.

1 80 feet (4c). Descend the slab to a line of holds on the right wall, which leads round an arête to a slab. Cross the slab and move up to a belay on the slab above (the belay at the start of Gorgeous Guano). This pitch can be avoided by descending the slab from the left side of the pillar (useful for high seas etc.).
2 60 feet (4b). Climb a crack to gain the groove on the right. Climb the groove to the overhang then move right into grooves. Belay as for A Separate Reality below the top of the pillar.
3 85 feet (5a). Traverse right to a spike. Climb the rightward-slanting crack for a few feet then go up a groove and follow a line of holds up to the right until it is possible to step up onto the large slab. Climb up to a peg belay in the centre of the slab. (Pitch 3 of A Separate Reality.)
4 35 feet. Make a slightly descending traverse right, passing below some large flakes, to a small ledge. Flake and nut belays high up.
5 150 feet (5a). Go up to a crack and follow it rightwards to an overhang. Pull round this then move right and follow a faint crack-line up to the right to a series of ledges. Follow these and belay some 20 feet from the top of the crag. Peg belays.
6 50 feet (4b). Traverse right along the ledge for ten feet and climb on widely-spaced holds to a crack, which leads to the top. Belay well back.

American Beauty 340 feet E1 (1975)
A superb route giving sustained slab climbing on excellent rock. Small to medium wire nuts are needed for protection. Retreat is quickly cut off by the tide although escape would probably be possible to the sides. Start some 20 feet right of the left-bounding groove.
1 40 feet (4a). Climb up for 10 feet then go diagonally right to a large ledge, nut belay.
2 90 feet (4c). Follow thin cracks bearing slightly left and continue in the same line to a boulder-strewn ledge, nut belays.
3 150 feet (5a/b). Climb the thin crack above to a narrow ledge and continue up the thinner cracks above with more difficulty to reach a good hold just left of a tongue of turf. Climb the thin parallel cracks above to the overhang then traverse right to a scoop where the roof is at its narrowest. Make a sharp pull to a good hold then traverse left, keeping low on clean rock until good holds lead up to belays at the foot of a steep corner.
4 60 feet (4c). Climb the corner and then bear left over vegetated slabs to the top.

BEAUFORT BUTTRESS   OS Ref. 1304 4629

The northern point of Jenny's Cove consists of: firstly a flat-topped rock island joined to the mainland at low tide, secondly a flat-topped buttress with a narrow 120-foot seaward face opposite the island, and thirdly a rather indistinct buttress. The climbs are on the 120-foot face of the flat-topped buttress.

The climbs on this cliff are rather slight and very close to each other, their first pitches having little real identity; however, both the rock and the situation are good.

Streaky   120 feet   Very Severe   (1979)
Start beneath the square-cut corner left of Hurricane.
1 40 feet (4c). Climb the corner to belay below a grey-streaked corner.
2 80 feet (4c). Climb the corner to the top.

Hurricane   120 feet   Severe   (1971)
Start below a shallow stepped corner 25 feet left of the central corner of Force Eight.
1 40 feet. Climb the corner to a belay at the foot of a green corner on the left of the main face.
2 45 feet. Step back onto the front face and climb the steep wall direct to a small ledge and flake belay.
3 35 feet. Continue more easily to the top.

Force Eight   120 feet   Severe   (1969)
Start at the foot of the shallow corner in the middle of the face.
1 45 feet. Climb the corner and go up to a ledge below the overhang.
2 75 feet. Climb the twin cracks above, passing the overhang, then go left to a ledge. Climb the crack moving right to finish.

Stuka   115 feet   Severe   (1969)
Start 5 feet right of the central corner of Force Eight.
1 45 feet. Climb a crack and then walls to the belay of Force Eight.
2 70 feet. Climb the corner on the right to the top.

Fifty Pumps   120 feet   Very Severe   (1979*)
Start 5 feet right of Stuka.
1 60 feet. Climb the obvious corner and then a groove to the overhang. Step right and go rightwards to a niche.
2 60 feet (4c). Climb the left hand crack above the niche to the top.

The next climb ventures into the narrow and steep-sided zawn immediately south of Beaufort Buttress. Descent is as for Beaufort Buttress and then by doubling back into the mouth of the zawn.

Salty Dog   160 feet   Very Difficult   (1979)
Work along the northern wall of the zawn until the way is barred by a rib. Start some 15 feet above the sea.
1 80 feet. Climb the left side of the rib until it is possible to step round the rib and traverse delicately right to a diagonal ramp. Follow the ramp to a good ledge halfway along. Nut belays.
2 80 feet. Continue along the ramp and finish up a steep corner.

DIHEDRAL ZAWN   OS Ref. 1308 4618

This is the small zawn 100 yards south of Beaufort Buttress. The next two climbs lie on the south side of the zawn. The easiest approach is to descend the rib south of the zawn and then traverse round into the zawn at half to low tide. A more adventurous low tide approach to Dihedral is to descend easy rock on the north side then to traverse into the zawn and to jump across to the south side at the narrowest point.

Dihedral   100 feet   E1   (1973)
The obvious big corner at the back in the south side, excellent holds and protection. Start by scrambling up to a spike belay 15 feet left of the corner.
1 100 feet (5a). Climb diagonally right into the corner, peg runner. Move up on small holds to gain the main corner crack, which is climbed to the top.

Illusion   105 feet   Severe   (1979*)
The obvious crack-line near the entrance to the zawn, some 100 feet right of Dihedral. Start beneath a short crack some 50 feet north of the descent.
1 15 feet. Climb up to a large ledge.
2 90 feet (4a). Climb the steep crack, awkwardly at first, until a slab is reached. Continue up the crack to the top. Good block belays.

PICNIC BAY CLIFF   OS Ref. 1314 4603

This is the short north-facing wall in a hidden bay just north of the Pyramid. Descent to the foot of the cliff is by Difficult standard climbing down the right hand side of the cliff (facing out) starting from the top of the Pyramid. Other descents are by abseil or at very low tide by scrambling around from the foot of the Pyramid. The climbs start from a platform with a small isolated pinnacle.

Sunday Morning 70 feet Very Severe (1976)
The clean-cut groove bounded by a cracked slab in the left side
of the wall. Start beneath the groove.
1 70 feet (4b). Climb slabs and step up to the foot of the groove.
Climb the groove or the crack in the slab on the left. Move left
to the finish.

Saturday Night 70 feet Severe (1976)
1 70 feet. Climb the dark-coloured groove at the back of the bay
on the right of the wall.

THE CHEESES OS Ref. 1333 4586 to 1327 4561
There are three buttresses at the end of the Halfway Wall, the
middle and largest buttress being about 120 feet high. Below the
southerly buttress is a similar buttress that rises from the top of
the sea level cliff below (the southerly section of Egyptian Slabs)—
it is possible to walk along the ledge at the foot of this buttress.

About 100 yards south of the Halfway Wall are two smaller
buttresses close together, the southerly of which has been called
the Cheesemite (OS Ref. 1335 4574). A further 100 yards south
is another bu'tress.

These buttresses give quite a lot of climbing but in general the
rock is poor and vegetated, and the climbing not particularly
enjoyable—except for on the Cheesemite, where the rock is
sounder but the climbs are less than 30 feet long.

EGYPTIAN SLABS OS Ref. 1325 4586
These lie beneath the Cheeses and extend for some 150 yards from
Box Zawn (OS Ref. 1325 4580), the small zawn immediately
north of Deep Zawn, to the small scruffy zawn beneath the end
of the Halfway Wall. The slabs are little over 100 feet high at
the southern end but rise to nearly 300 feet at the northern end.

The first climb is approached by scrambling down the grass
slopes immediately north of the Halfway Wall and then abseiling
down a broken chossy slope to the easy rock spur just north of
the small scruffy zawn.

Pathfinder 300 feet Hard Very Severe (1974)
A climb up the highest section of the slabs, near the left end. A
feature of the climb is the small stances and poor belays, for
which a fair selection of blade pegs are advisable. Start on the
boulders in the zawnbed, below a wide chimney just left of the
slabs.

1 45 feet. Climb the chimney to a large boulder and flake belay.
2 85 feet (4a). Traverse up to the right for some 30 feet to the foot of a short rib. Climb the rib, starting on its right side, to a narrow ledge, peg runner. Move left to a broken groove, which is climbed to a small stance and peg belay at the point where the groove merges into the slab above.
3 40 feet (4c). Climb up above the stance to gain the left end of a narrow broken ledge. Traverse right, beneath the obvious white slab, to the spacious ledge at the foot of the large overhung recess, peg belay.
4 80 feet (5a). Move back left to gain the spur left of the recess and climb steeply up to the left onto the prominent white slab, peg runner (in place). Climb cracks in the slab to narrow ledges beneath the final groove, peg belays.
5 50 feet (5a). Climb cracks in the left wall of the groove to join the groove above a small overhang, peg runner (in place). Follow the groove to the top, belay well back.

Below the lichen-covered tower that forms the lowest of the Cheeses is an area of broken rock separated from Box Zawn by a smooth narrow slab. The next two climbs are to the left of the broken rock and lie on the smooth yellow-streaked slab capped by an overhang above its left side. The approach is by abseil from the foot of the lower Cheese to the large sea level ledges below the broken rock. The deceptively easy-looking area of broken rock can be climbed at Very Difficult to Severe standard.

Immaculate Slab   110 feet   Very Severe   (1974)
A really excellent pitch on perfect rock up the left side of the slab and immediately beneath the overhanging retaining wall. Sustained and quite hard for its grade. Start on the narrow ledge beneath the slab. At low tide a pleasant 20-foot pitch can be made up the wall below the ledge.
1 110 feet (4c). From the left end of the narrow ledge, move up into a very shallow groove, which leads up to the slab below the overhang. Follow a line up to the right beneath the retaining wall to a final short steep section, which is entered from a large foothold on the right. Peg belay on a large flat ledge. Scramble to the top.

The Gem   100 feet   Hard Very Severe   (1974*)
A line near the right edge of the slab with a technically hard entry well protected by small nuts. Start from the narrow ledge below the slab.
1 100 feet (5c). Climb the short steep wall some 10 feet left of the right arête and just left of an overhang to gain the main slab.

Move right and climb the slab to the final steeper section then go back left and climb a short crack finishing by a flake. Peg belay on the smooth ledge above Immaculate Slab. Scramble to the top.

The next two climbs lie on the smooth narrow slab immediately north of Box Zawn.

Live Gold   125 fee.   Very Severe   (1974*)
Start on the sloping ledge below the left side of the slab, just above the sea.
1 45 feet (4c). Climb up to the right into an obvious V-chimney. Climb this and exit left onto the slab. Climb up and left to a good ledge, peg and nut belay.
2 80 feet (4b). Climb cracks in the slab finishing up a corner with a large jammed block in it. Large block belay. Scramble to the top.

Limey   110 feet   Very Severe   (1974*)
Start by traversing beneath the foot of the slab, past a square rib, to a large ledge almost in Box Zawn.
1 40 feet (4c). Right of the rib is a corner whose left wall forms the right edge of the slab. Climb the corner to where it steepens and pull out left onto a small ledge on the slab. Climb up to a white ledge, nut belays.
2 70 feet (4a). Climb cracks in the slab to the top. Scramble off.

The next climb is actually in Box Zawn though it is very near Limey.

Jack-in-the-Box   140 feet   Very Severe   (1975*)
The obvious right hand groove of the two in the north side of the zawn.
1 140 feet. Enter the groove from the left and climb it direct.

DEEP ZAWN   OS Ref. 1324 4574
Deep Zawn provides a concentrated collection of the hardest, best and most serious climbs on the island—the fact that all of the routes are in the Extreme grade is no coincidence. The routes that start from the zawnbed are particularly serious since retreat is cut off at half tide and there are no easy escape routes.

The zawn is the first zawn north of the Devil's Chimney (about 75 yards). As its name implies, it is very deep and is also narrow for its full length with high steep side and back walls. A small stream runs down into the zawn from the smaller Cheeses about 100 yards south of the Halfway Wall.

To approach the foot of the zawn, descend the arête formed by the top of its north side until it steepens and a faint track leads rightwards (facing out) to an abseil point marked by pointed blocks. Descend to big ledges near sea level—this can be climbed at Very Difficult standard. The ledges are above high water and they extend into the zawn along the base of the north wall as far as Antiworlds, the slanting groove line in the centre of the wall. From here a short abseil to the zawnbed gives access to Creation, The Stone Tape and Underworld at half tide—at low tide, a descent can be made to the boulders at the mouth of the zawn.

The Serpent   160 feet   E1   (1973)
A bold and strenuous climb whose main pitch takes the obvious snaking crack line near the seaward edge of the north wall. Start on the ledges beneath the arête of the wall.
1 70 feet (4a). Climb the groove just left of the arête for 40 feet then move right and up ledges on the rib to a stance at the pointed block.
2 90 feet (5a). Move up right to ledges and climb the crack above to the top—the narrowest section at 30 feet being the hardest.

Supernova   200 feet   E3   (1973)
Very fingery and technical climbing up the thin crack in the sheer wall right of the snaking crack of The Serpent. Start just right of the seaward edge of the wall.
1 60 feet (5c). Climb the rib left of a black wall then step right to the foot of a thin crack. Use a peg for aid to start a series of hard moves up the wall to reach a good edge, which leads to a stance beneath an overhanging corner. Nut belay.
2 40 feet (4b). Climb the corner and up to ledges on the right. Move right along these for 15 feet to a peg belay beneath the thin crack.
3 100 feet (6a). Climb the crack, using a wire sling at 25 feet and a peg at 55 feet for aid, and the shallow finishing corners to the top.

Quatermass   200 feet   E2   (1973)
A very fine route centred on the conspicuous parallel cracks left of the slanting groove line of Antiworlds. Start where the crack line extends down to the ledges at the base of the wall.
1 80 feet (5b). Climb leftwards into a scoop then step up left and climb the thin crack on the right to gain a small incut ledge on the right with difficulty. Continue to an overhang, peg runner, and go straight up for 25 feet then move right along small ledges,

past a dubious flake, to the halfway ledge. Peg and nut belays beneath the parallel cracks.

2 40 feet (5a). Climb the cracks to another good ledge.

3 80 feet (4b). Continue pleasantly up the stepped corner to the top.

Antiworlds 245 feet E3 (1972)
A superb route up the obvious rightward-slanting grooves finishing up thin cracks in the blank-looking wall above. Serious, sustained on excellent rock and with good protection. Start where the ledges end, peg belay.

1 110 feet (5c). Use tension from the belay to reach a crack system on the right and climb steeply up this to small ledges at the foot of the big groove. Climb a thin slanting crack on the right for 15 feet then the groove itself to where a smooth fin of rock divides it—small wire nut just below the fin. Climb up past the fin by hard moves until it is possible to swing out right and up to better holds. Continue more easily to a stance and peg belays.

2 70 feet (5c). Climb the corner above until it begins to bulge. Continue with increasing difficulty until excellent holds at the top of the corner can be reached. Climb up to the left for a few feet to a good stance and peg belays.

3 65 feet (5a). Move down right until beneath the thin parallel cracks. Follow the crack line to the top, using a wire sling for aid low down and then two aid pegs after the thin horizontal slot.

Creation 280 feet E2 (1973)
A climb of great character up the huge crack line in the right side of the north wall. The first pitch is strenuous, intimidating and will always be wet in places; the second pitch is easier but is a serious lead with some poor rock. Start at around low tide on the zawnbed below the crack.

1 120 feet (5b). Follow the crack to a small stance above the large overhang. Peg (large angle) belay.

2 90 feet (5a). Continue in the same line to a smooth shallow section of the crack. Move up and then right with some difficulty to reach excellent holds, which lead to a stance. Blade peg belays.

3 70 feet (4b). Continue up the crack-line until above a shallow chimney then traverse left and up to the top.

The Stone Tape   315 feet   E3   (1973)

A magnificent route which epitomises zawn climbing. It mainly follows the left edge of the steep slab that forms the back of the zawn. Start at around low tide at the foot of the south wall some 20 feet right of the wet chimney-line that forms the lower part of the junction between the south and back walls of the zawn.

1 90 feet (5b). Climb to a spike then move left and up a shallow groove to a ledge, which is gained at its right end. Climb straight up to a stepped groove, which leads to a large ledge. Continue up the corner to another ledge beneath the big slab in the back of the zawn. The lower half of this pitch will always be damp.

2 65 feet (5b/c). Climb up for 15 feet to a thin crack in the black slab. Climb the crack with difficulty for a further 15 feet to a peg and sling in situ. Make a tension traverse leftwards to a good foothold at the bottom of the groove/crack-line that descends to the lowest point of the slab. In abnormally dry conditions the tension traverse can be avoided by a rising traverse to gain the crack at a higher point. Follow the crack to a tiny ledge beneath overhangs. Peg belays.

3 40 feet (5b). Step left and move up to stand on a flake. Climb the groove with difficulty then move onto the right wall and climb up until the groove can be recrossed using an incut flake on its left wall. Belay a few feet above on a small ledge by a good half-inch crack.

4 120 feet (4c). Continue up the groove to the narrow grassy ledge that crosses the slab (no belay). Climb the slab direct to the obvious shallow grooves, which are followed bearing left where they peter out. More grooves lead to a short final slab, after which 15 feet of grass lead to a huge block belay.

Underworld   200 feet   E3   (1973)

The most striking line on the south wall is a smooth greenish groove, more or less in the centre of the wall. This provides a superb pitch which is entered by a precarious and acrobatic traverse beneath a line of overhangs. Start in the zawnbed below the start of the traverse-line.

1 20 feet. Climb up to a cave.

2. 40 feet (5c). Traverse right beneath the overhangs to reach an excellent crack after a very thin section. Move round the nose to a small stance and nut belays beneath the smooth groove.

3 90 feet (5c). Climb the groove to a small stance on the left arête. Peg belay.

4 50 feet (5a). Climb the groove above and continue to the top.

Genesis   130 feet   E1   (1978*)
The obvious chimney/groove line 40 feet right of Underworld,
inferior to the other Deep Zawn routes. Start by abseiling to a
spike at the foot of the line.
1 130 feet (5b). Climb up into the chimney. Climb this and over
an overhang to gain the crack above, which is followed to easier
ground and the top.

THE DEVIL'S CHIMNEY AREA
The approach, which can be used up to half tide at least for the
Chimney itself, is by descending the steep rib of boulders and
grass on the south side of the Devil's Chimney Zawn and south
east of the Devil's Chimney itself. The best approach to the top
of the rib is by traversing onto it from the south (left facing out).

THE DEVIL'S CHIMNEY CLIFF   OS Ref. 1320 4568
Immediately inland of the Devil's Chimney is the impressive
undercut wall of the Devil's Chimney Cliff. This is bounded on
its right by a grassy gully and on its left by Deep Zawn.

To the left of the wide fault line which defines the left edge of
the main section of the cliff is a clean white wall, which gives
three routes. The left-bounding arête of the white wall (which is
also the south arête of Deep Zawn) is rounded and contains a
number of corner and groove lines. Sliver takes the very slim
groove on the very edge of the arête while Tindale Route takes
the slabby corner on the right side of the arête.

Sliver   80 feet   Very Severe   (1978*)
An interesting pitch on excellent rock, harder than it looks.
Start on a ledge beneath the slim groove.
1 80 feet (5a). Follow the groove to the top and scramble to a
belay.

Tindale Route   90 feet   Very Severe   (1965*)
Start on the ledges below the arête.
1 15 feet. Climb a short steep wall to the ledge below the corner.
2 75 feet. Climb the corner for 60 feet to a peg, which is used for
aid. Use another peg for aid 8 feet higher then make an awkward
traverse right to the edge, which is followed for a few feet to a
good belay. Scramble to the top.

Peyote   130 feet   Hard Very Severe   (1974*)
A good, well-positioned climb taking a series of grooves in the
left arête of the white wall. Start on seaweed-covered ledges left
of a small overhang some 25 yards left of the right edge of the
white wall.

1 130 feet (4c). Climb the groove behind the belay with a small nut for aid to a line of holds leading to the arête on the right, peg runner. Follow the line to the right then climb a small open corner to a small overhang. Use a peg for aid in a blank slab then trend left back into the obvious groove, which is climbed to the top.

The Fifth Appendage   180 feet   Hard Very Severe   (1973)
Delicate climbing in good situations. Start as for Peyote.
1 70 feet (5a). Scramble across seaweed-covered slabs beneath an overhang to a rightward-facing groove, peg runner. Climb the groove until a delicate traverse right leads to small ledges, peg runner. Move right again for a few feet then trend up and left to a small stance and peg belays.
2 110 feet (4c). Climb the slab behind the stance to overhangs. Continue directly over the first overhang and turn the second on the right. Move up and left to a good flake then follow the crack on the right to finish.

The Reluctant Teamaker   170 feet   Very Severe and A1   (1973*)
The obvious corner in the right side of the white wall.
1 60 feet (5a A1). Peg up the corner for 20 feet (4 pegs). Free climb up to and over the large overhang, turning it on the left. Continue up the crack to a ledge and traverse left onto the slab to a stance.
2 110 feet (4b). Climb diagonally left across slabs below the obvious rake to finish on a large ledge.

The main section of the Devil's Chimney Cliff, immediately behind the Devil's Chimney, is one of the most impressive cliffs on the island. Some 20 yards left of the right hand bounding gully is a steep gully/groove fault line that curves over to the left; Overlord, the original and easiest climb on this section of the cliff, crosses and recrosses the fault line to finish up the steep slabs forming the upper section of the wall. The Promised Land and Stalingrad force entries through the overhanging rock left of Overlord and immediately behind the Devil's Chimney. The other two routes, Diablo and Spacewalk, climb the overhangs directly above the spur of Overlord's second pitch.

The Promised Land   280 feet   E2   (1974)
A magnificent route which climbs improbable-looking rock on reasonable holds—protection is excellent and all pegs are in place. Start about 30 yards left of Overlord, at a line of holds beneath a corner 25 feet up.

1 100 feet (5b). Climb up for 10 feet then step left and climb directly up the black slab into grooves leading up to the big overhang. Traverse left for 20 feet on good incuts, some wet rock, to a point beneath the left side of the huge block on the lip of the overhang. Pull up to gain a chimneying position beside the block and move out right using the crack above it to peg belays above the roof.

2 50 feet (5b). Climb the groove above until holds run out into blank rock. Swing out right using a peg handhold then climb easily up to the right to a stance (on Stalingrad).

3 130 feet (5a). Climb the crack above to reach a big spike on the right then climb diagonally right to a jug-rimmed ledge. Climb the groove above for 20 feet to a cluster of spikes then traverse right on good holds to another groove, which leads to the top.

Stalingrad 270 feet E3 (1974)
A strong natural line with a very fierce entry and finishing up the obvious crack system in the left side of the upper wall. Start as for The Promised Land, beneath the corner 25 feet up.

1 100 feet (5c). Climb up bearing right then pull up left to the base of the corner. Climb the corner to the edge of a small slab then traverse right very thinly across the slab and move up into a crack. Move strenuously rightwards to a spike and follow the basalt fault line to a small stance, nut belays.

2 50 feet (4a). Climb the crack then move left and up a series of steps in the slab to a stance beneath the distinctive crack.

3 120 feet (5a). Climb the steep crack and continue directly to the top.

Overlord 360 feet Hard Very Severe (1972)
A serious route of great character taking the easiest line through a very impressive area of rock. It begins by climbing up to the right of the main fault line near the right end of the cliff and then makes a crucial leftward traverse to gain the upper slabs, which give a delectable pitch. Anything other than dry conditions can make the lower pitches much harder and quite nasty. Start 10 yards left of the fault line below a wide crack, which is inaccessible at high tide.

1 30 feet. Climb the crack to a ledge.

2 100 feet (5a). Climb up to the right and cross the fault line to gain a greenish slab in the spur on the right. Move across the foot of the slab into a shallow groove, which leads to a ledge. Continue up the spur on suspect rock, trending slightly left, to a stance on its top. Multiple belays recommended.

3 80 feet (4c). Move left into the fault line, now a gully, and descend until moves left can be made onto the obvious traverse line, peg runner. Step up and traverse left along the upper line of flakes to a large pointed block, peg runner. Climb a short steep wall and follow another line of flakes leftwards to a stance on the edge of the large slab, peg belays.

4 150 feet (4b). Step up left and climb the crack-line in the slab to holds leading rightwards to short cracks. Climb these then move left to the obvious wide crack, which leads to the top. Scramble to belays.

Diablo   280 feet   E2   (1974*)

A gloomy but worthwhile route. Technical difficulty is not high but many holds are suspect and the line is intimidating. Start as for Overlord.

1 130 feet (5a). As for the first two pitches of Overlord but take a stance on the right. Good belays on huge spikes.

2 80 feet (5b). Move up and swing right using an apparently solid detached column of rock. Climb the groove above until a sharp flake on the left wall is reached then move right and up to a poor stance, high nut belays.

3 70 feet (4c). Move up left and climb the slab to the top.

Spacewalk   280 feet   E2   (1974)

Excellent climbing in an exceptionally exposed position on good rock throughout. It takes the rib right of the spur of Overlord and then climbs the edge of the huge impending central fault by a series of grooves. Start beneath the rib.

1 130 feet (5b). Climb the right side of the rib to a ledge. Continue up the steep groove above and then up the arête until delicate climbing gains a stance, peg belays.

2 80 feet (5a/b). The groove just left of the stance is climbed until after some 15 feet a move left can be made to good holds on a rib. Climb up to enter the groove of Diablo and go up this for a few feet until standing on a big flake on the right wall. Traverse left across the wall on flat holds to gain a larger, bottomless groove, which is climbed for 10 feet to a small stance and nut belays.

3 70 feet (5a/b). Climb the groove, and then move left and up to the obvious line of holds on the exposed wall. Climb vertically to a ledge then bear slightly left to finish.

The Mexican Connection   475 feet   Hard Very Severe   (1974*)

A serious route with good situations; it girdles the cliff from left to right, starting up Fifth Appendage and finishing up Overlord. Start as for Fifth Appendage and Peyote.

1 70 feet (5a). As for Fifth Appendage, move right beneath the overhang then take a diagonal line up to the right starting up a rightward-facing groove. Small stance and peg belays.

2 85 feet (4b). Make a rising traverse along a line of good holds to a ledge in a corner. Continue in the same line to a stance on the edge of the gully.

3 80 feet (5a). Move up grooves and ledges above the stance until it is possible to traverse into the gully. Move out onto a rib on the other side of the gully and step up to a ledge, peg runner. Traverse right for 10 feet and make a hard move into a scoop. Climb the wall above with 3 pegs for aid and move right to a ledge.

4 45 feet (4a). Traverse right to a stance on Stalingrad and descend 25 feet of that climb, down steps in the slab to the right.

5 35 feet (4c). Move across the crack-line and make a series of delicate moves to gain another crack on the right. Follow this for a few feet until it is possible to make a long step right onto the ledge below the last pitch of Overlord.

6 150 feet (4b). Follow Overlord to the top, by climbing the obvious crack system.

THE DEVIL'S CHIMNEY   OS Ref. 1319 4570
Descent is by abseil.

White Riot   130 feet   Very Severe   (1979*)
Start beneath the west face.

1 60 feet (4c). Climb the small crack right of the main crack to an overhang then move right and follow cracks in the wall to the large ledge on the ordinary route.

2 70 feet (4c). Step onto the slab above the left edge of the ledge and move left onto the west face. Move up with difficulty onto a flat-topped pinnacle then go right and finish up cracked blocks on the right.

The Devils Chimney   105 feet   Very Severe   (1961/1969)
A good climb in dramatic surroundings up the largest of the island's pinnacles. Start on the south side, opposite the descent rib, by scrambling up an easy rib to the foot of a pair of steep cracks to the right of the south face.

1 35 feet (4a). Climb the right hand crack then traverse easily left to a large boulder-strewn ledge.

2 70 feet (4c). Climb the centre of the steep slab above by a thin crack to a small overhang. Climb the overhang and the steep wall above, trending left to the arête, which is followed to the summit.

Variation   The Original Finish   70 feet   Very Severe
2a 70 feet. Climb a steep groove formed by a small pinnacle at
the extreme left edge of the south face and continue up the
arête to the top. Loose.

THE DEVIL'S TOWER   OS Ref. 1316 4563
This is the very impressive, narrow tower that overlooks the
Devil's Chimney—between the Devil's Chimney Cliff and the
way down.

Hob's Lane   90 feet   E1   (1974*)
The obvious crack in the face overlooking the way down. The
foot of the crack is approach by ascending the gully beneath the
face or by making a short abseil from the way down.
1 90 feet (5b). Climb the crack to a thread belay at the top.
Varied nuts needed for protection.

PUNCHBOWL CLIFF   OS Ref. 1308 4564
Between the Devil's Chimney and Needle Rock, some 100 yards
from the former, is an obvious arête rising almost from the sea.
There are faces either side of this arête.

The cliff can be approached at lowish tide by a sea level traverse
from the Devil's Chimney, or by a longer and somewhat tedious
traverse from Needle Rock. A more direct approach to The
Green Light is provided by a straightforward 140-foot abseil
down the wall to the south of that climb from large blocks at the
top.

The first route lies on the north side of the cliff, on the wall
facing the Devil's Chimney.

Round the Horn   150 feet   Very Severe (1974)
A prominent projecting finger of rock in the centre of the face
provides the focal point of the climb. Some loose rock. Start at
the foot of a groove 20 feet right of the crack leading directly to
the finger.
1 90 feet (4b). Climb the groove until it steepens into loose
blocks and it is possible to traverse left to belay on the finger.
2 60 feet (4a). Step left to a groove, which is followed to the top.

Punchbowl Arête   130 feet   Very Difficult   (1969)
The obvious arête provides a pleasant way up from the sea level
boulders.
1 130 feet. Follow the arête more or less directly, the main
difficulty being provided by a short smooth groove halfway up
which is entered from the left. Some loose rock.

The south section of the cliff, to the right of Punchbowl Arête, faces due west and is bounded on its right by the stream running down from Punchbowl Valley. A line of overhangs cross the face at two thirds height—below the overhangs the rock is clean and above, lichen-covered.

The Green Light   130 feet   Hard Very Severe   (1973*)
A fine climb up the large tapering chimney in the left side of the face. There is a distinct lack of belays at the top and it may be worth leaving a fixed rope from higher up the slope.
1 130 feet (5a). Climb the chimney, exiting right onto a short slab, then step left across the chimney to some small ledges. Climb the steep wall just left of a crack to more ledges. Climb a crack leading easily off to the left for a few moves until a thin crack on the right can be gained and followed to a small overlap. Climb this with difficulty and then the wall to the top.

THE EARTHQUAKE   OS Ref. 1305 4546
The Earthquake runs north/south across the top of the ridge leading down to Needle Rock. The most westerly cleft is about 5 feet wide; its deepest part is the southerly half, the northerly part being much shallower. An earthy scramble can be made through the base of the cleft.

A number of climbs, mostly on friable rock, can be made at Very Difficult to Severe standard up the cracks in the side walls. The most substantial climb is **Epicentre** (90 feet, Hard Severe), which takes the crack in the left wall when entering from the south starting from the lowest point of the floor.

Below the cleft, the prominent pinnacle on the arête leading down to Needle Rock and the spur beneath it provide a number of short pitches.

NEEDLE ROCK   OS Ref. 1292 4557
Descent to Needle Rock is left to the individual since the direct approach down the slopes just south of the ridge leading down to the Rock is very steep for scrambling but it can be used. Further south the descent is better, down the obvious rake (towards Bomber Buttress), but the subsequent traverse back to Needle Rock across slimy boulders is tiring and only possible at low tide. The boulders leading out to the Rock can be crossed at most states of the tide but there are times when they are under water.

The Ordinary Route   65 feet   Difficult   (1961)
A delightful climb on sound rock. Start from the seaward end
of the large flat platform below the north face.
1 40 feet. Make an awkward step up to the right onto the seaward
face. Climb diagonally up to the right to a large ledge.
2 25 feet. Move back right onto the face and climb it to the top.
This pitch can be avoided on the left.

Descent from the summit is down steps on the north face to a
ledge with a flake on the north west arête. From here an abseil
leads to the starting platform. Alternatively, the lower part of
the Ordinary Route can be reversed, only the bottom move being
at all difficult.

It is possible to climb directly up to the ledge with the abseil
flake by a wall at a Very Difficult standard. Another short pitch
is given by the short steep layback-corner in the north west
aspect of the Rock, **Thread** (20 feet, Severe)

The seaward face of the Rock is steep and covered with excellent
holds, and it is possible to make a number of lines between the
Ordinary Route and Integrity. However, the latter as described
is the best line.

Integrity   80 feet   Severe   (1967)
For its standard and length, a most enjoyable climb in excellent
position. Start at the foot of the south west arête of the Rock.
1 80 feet. Climb round to the left onto the seaward face and
climb a crack 6 feet left of the arête for 25 feet. Move right to the
arête then climb up to a knife edge spur in the arête. Move up
on large holds and move right onto the south face, which is
climbed via a large finishing flake.

The Obverse Route   80 feet   Hard Severe   (1965)
Start below the landward side of the rock.
1 45 feet. Climb up to the narrow rake running from left to
right and follow this on small holds to a large ledge.
2 35 feet. Climb two short walls then up to the summit.

BOMBER BUTTRESS AREA
About 200 yards south of Needle Rock is a squat triangular
pinnacle joined to the mainland by a large boulder-bridge. This is
opposite the foot of the wide rake leading down from the north
and is immediately below a prominent plateau-level outcrop with
outward-jutting blocks which form a face-like profile.

Bomber Buttress is the steep north-facing cliff above the foot of
the rake and Banana Buttress is the smaller slabby buttress
opposite the squat pinnacle and underneath the foot of the rake.

The third cliff in this area, Fighter Buttress, is some 40 yards to the south.

Descent to these cliffs is down the rake. At its foot, the best descent then continues down sea level tunnels, the Tunnels of Lovely, formed by the massive boulders either to the right (facing in) to Bomber Buttress or to the left to Banana Buttress. The first climb lies to the north of Banana Buttress:

Lemon Pie   110 feet   Hard Very Severe   (1977*)
Start 10 yards north of the basalt dyke.
1 110 feet (5a). Climb the right edge of the obvious triangular slab to a ledge at 20 feet. Climb the groove above the ledge and move right onto a slab to finish.

BANANA BUTTRESS   OS Ref. 1290 4537
This gives some pleasant climbing. The obvious central line is **Mellow Yellow** (100 feet, Difficult), which starts 20 yards left of the jammed boulder on the right of the face and goes up to the right to the large ledge 25 feet up; it then goes left to follow an obvious line up cracks and slabs to the top. Two harder climbs, **Banana Split** (100 feet, Hard Severe) and **Banana Crack** (90 feet, Severe), take lines from the large ledge to the left and right of Mellow Yellow respectively. The large ledge can also be approached from the right to provide a harder start to either of these climbs.

BOMBER BUTTRESS   OS Ref. 1288 4534
The buttress slants up to the left and the climbs start at two levels. The first two climbs start from the large boulders above the Tunnels of Lovely below the fiercely steep wall of Bender with the striking impending crack of Jetset on the right. Right again is a steep broken corner that is the central feature of the face. The other routes start lower down on the right below the Tunnels of Lovely and near the right edge of the face.

Bender   120 feet   E2   (1973)
A fine climb, sustained and strenuous, taking the large curving crack in the main overhanging wall in the left hand section of the face. Start at the large boulder stance beneath the wall.
1 120 feet (5c). Climb the smooth wall on the left to a crack. Climb this until a difficult step right can be made into the wide crack, which leads up to an overhang. Move right beneath the overhang and then up a good crack on the right to a ramp, which is followed for a few feet to a resting position. Step up left and climb deep cracks to a wider section. Continue up cracks then traverse left, past a large chockstone, to a ramp. Climb the

ramp to an overhang then move up into the overhanging crack on the right. Climb the crack and continue steeply to the top.

Jetset   100 feet   E1   (1973)
A very impressive climb of good quality up the obvious crack. Strenuous and sustained but well protected. Start at the boulder beneath the crack.
1 100 feet (5a). Enter the crack above the first overhang and follow it over three overhangs to the top.

Quandary   210 feet   Very Severe   (1973)
A pleasant climb taking a diagonal line from right to left beneath the main wall of the cliff up slabs and walls. Start at the boulders at the bottom of the Tunnels of Lovely.
1 60 feet (4a). Climb the rightward-slanting ramp to a corner. Make a strenuous pull into a niche then step right and go up behind a flake. Step left at the top and traverse 10 feet left to the large boulder stance beneath Jetset and Bender.
2 75 feet (4b). Climb the slab above for 15 feet then climb a ramp to a steep section, which is climbed strenuously to a good stance. Peg belay.
3 75 feet (4a). Move up right to a blank groove. Climb the layback-flake on the right wall then hand traverse left and up back to the gully above, peg runner, and continue to the top.

Flashback   115 feet   Very Severe   (1973*)
This takes a corner to the boulder stance in the centre of the face and finishes up the overhanging prow above. Start at the bottom of the Tunnels of Lovely, below a chimney.
1 75 feet (4b). Climb the short chimney then the corner above to a small overhang, old peg runner. Step up left into the wide crack and follow it to the boulder stance.
2 40 feet (4b). Climb the overhanging wall on the right with two pegs for aid to a niche. Climb the crack on the right to the top.

Beamsplitter   110 feet   Hard Very Severe   (1973*)
The crack right of the corner of Flashback is followed by the wide crack in the wall on the right. Start at the bottom of the Tunnels of Lovely.
1 60 feet (4a). Climb the short chimney then the crack to a small stance on the right, peg belay.
2 50 feet (5b). Traverse right across a slab to the thin crack. Climb this and the wider crack above to a ledge. Finish up a short corner.

The next climb lies on the rock between Bomber and Fighter Buttresses:

Biggles   120 feet   Very Difficult   (1976)
A pleasant climb up the slabs and grooves between the two buttresses.
1 50 feet. Climb the lower slab to a ledge beneath a groove.
2 70 feet. Climb up just right of the groove and continue to the top.

FIGHTER BUTTRESS   OS Ref. 1284 4532
This is the smaller counterpart of Bomber Buttress, 40 yards to its south. It is similar in appearance, facing north and slanting up to the left. Access is possible at all states of the tide, the cliff being approached either by a sea level traverse from Bomber Buttress or by a traverse north from Dead Cow Point.

The right hand section of the cliff is formed by a steep wall with a crack-line on either side, which are the bases for the two routes on the cliff. Loose rock on the top pitches of both climbs can make them potentially dangerous undertakings.

The best belay at the top of the cliff is a good thread some 15 yards above the centre of the cliff. Due to the loose nature of the terrain above the cliff the belay is best approached by making a detour over to the right.

Tracer   100 feet   Very Severe   (1973*)
The central crack left of the steep wall. Start below a groove leading up to the crack.
1 60 feet (4c). Climb the groove and the crack above to ledges on the left, peg belays.
2 40 feet (4a). Step back right and climb the crack to the top.

Flak   100 feet   Very Severe   (1973*)
Start below the right hand crack.
1 100 feet (4c). Climb the crack to the point where it becomes a corner. Step left onto a ledge and move along the ledge for 15 feet into the centre of the face, which is climbed to the top.

BEEF BUTTRESS   OS Ref. 1284 4512
This is the small steep south-facing cliff on the southern flank of Dead Cow Point; it forms the northern wall of the boulder beach directly below the Quarter Wall. The foot of the cliff is approached by a 200-foot abseil down the cliff itself from good blocks well above the top of the cliff. The boulder beach can also be reached by a steep scramble down from the Quarter Wall.

The most prominent central feature of the cliff is the large high cave formed by two vertical dykes. To the left of the cave is a wide steep wall of good rock with the sharp overhang of The Vice at two thirds height and immediately left of the cave.

The Vice   150 feet   Hard Very Severe   (1973*)
A fine climb taking a a line up and then out of the left
side of the large cave. Start just left of the left arête of the cave,
below a thin crack leading to a small groove.
1 100 feet (5a). Climb the cracks with two pegs for aid and gain
the left edge of the groove. Climb this for 6 feet then step across
the groove to a small ledge on the arête. Climb up rightwards to
a downward-pointing fang under the roof of the cave. Using the
fang make a difficult move left to good holds above the overhang.
Continue through a narrow gap in the overhang above to a
stance and nut belays.
2 50 feet. Finish up the corner above. Scramble to good blocks
well back.

Spanner   100 feet   Very Severe   (1979*)
Start some 60 feet right of The Vice below an obvious slabby
corner.
1 100 feet (4c). Climb the corner, poor protection, to an
awkward mantelshelf at 50 feet. Finish up the broken groove
just left of the arête. Block and nut belay.

FLYING BUTTRESS AREA   OS Ref. 1272 4489
A small easily-accessible cliff with impressive rock architecture. It
gives a number of good short routes and one small cliff classic
in Diamond Solitaire.

From the Battery descend towards the south down steep broken
rock. About 30 feet above the sea return to the north, scrambling
over boulders to the foot of the Flying Buttress, which leans up
against the main cliff with a colossal arch underneath. The foot
of the buttress itself is only accessible one and a half hours either
side of low water. However the Flying Buttress can be descended
without much difficulty. The climbing lies on the Flying Buttress
itself and on the cliffs on either side. The climbs on the south
side of the buttress are accessible at most states of the tide.·

The mainland cliff north of the Flying Buttress is approached
at less than high tide by traversing under the arch on barnacle-
encrusted rock. The left limit of the cliff is a broken buttress just
left of a prominent rib, Battery Rib. The broken buttress gives a
scrambling climb with a short steep wall at the top—to the left
are some short pitches at Very Difficult. At high tide this broken
buttress can be used to approach Battery Rib. To the left of the
broken buttress is the entrance to a tunnel cutting through the
headland to emerge opposite St. Patrick's Buttress.

Battery Rib   110 feet   Very Difficult   (1965)
A very enjoyable little climb, steep with large holds, up the
prominent rib. Start in a recess just left of the foot of the rib.
1 70 feet. Climb up the recess until it is possible to traverse
right to the rib. Climb the steep left wall of the rib on huge holds
then move onto the edge of the rib, which leads to a belay.
2 40 feet. Climb the rib to the top, various lines possible.

Vallum   110 feet   Severe   (1973)
Start beneath the V-chimney just right of Battery Rib.
1 70 feet. Enter the chimney direct or from the right about 10
feet up and follow it to a stance and belay on Battery Rib.
2 40 feet. Step right and climb the cracked wall to the top.

Variation Finish   50 feet   Hard Severe   (1975)
2a 50 feet. Descend from the belay until a step right can be made
to a ledge. Climb a crack up the left side of the slab to a corner,
which is followed to the top.

On the Flying Buttress itself:

The Flying Buttress   170 feet   Moderate   (1962)   6/9/8? ↓
A pleasant, though rather broken, climb. Starting beneath the
left edge of the buttress, either trend right or go up the left edge
to a broken section at half height. From here various lines are
possible up the steeper top section.

Horseman's Route   160 feet   Hard Severe   (1964)   6/9/8? + T.E
A wandering line which gives varied and interesting climbing.
Start about 40 feet right of the Flying Buttress route, below a
50-foot slab.
1 80 feet (4a). Climb the middle of the slab and continue to a
belay on the broken halfway ledge.
2 80 feet (4a). Step down to the right onto the steep smooth
slab of Diamond Solitaire. Make an ascending traverse to the
right across the slab to a ledge. Climb up to the left to black-
streaked rock and continue over lichen-covered blocks then
scramble to the top.

Diamond Solitaire   160 feet   Very Severe   (1965)
A magnificent little climb—the excellent rock and position more
than compensate for the fact that one can deviate almost at will
from the line (hence the variations). It takes the impressive 120-
foot slab in the right flank of the Flying Buttress. Start below
the slab at lowish tide.

1 20 feet. Climb the steep rough crack to belay in the cave at the foot of the slab.
2 65 feet (4c). Move out right onto the slab and climb the first 15 feet of the slab with difficulty using the corner as required. Continue up the corner and move left to belay on the halfway ledge on the Flying Buttress route.
3 75 feet (4a). Traverse right on the slab for 10 feet. Climb directly up the middle of the slab and trend right where it steepens near the top to finish.

Variations
The whole climb can be made more sustained after the first 15 feet by climbing direct up the centre of the slab and by running the two pitches together.

The next climbs lie on the mainland cliff south of the Flying Buttress. The most obvious feature is the depression of broken rock, between 60 and 30 feet wide, whose curving left side is overlooked by an impending wall. The impending wall has been climbed as an artifical climb.

Capuccino 135 feet Hard Severe (1963)
A slight climb with some interesting moves in its top pitch. Start below the left corner of the depression.
1 85 feet. Climb the corner and move right to a good stance.
2 50 feet (4c). Climb the small bulge on the left then take a diagonal line up to the left beneath the overhang. Move left to broken rock, which leads to the top.

Variation **Direct Finish** 60 feet Very Severe (1975*)
2a 60 feet. Climb the bulge as for the ordinary route then traverse right to a large ledge. Climb the thin crack on the left using two pegs for aid to a small ledge on the left beneath an overhang. Climb the overhang with one nut for aid then trend right to finish.

Alouette 110 feet Difficult (1963)
Start below the right hand corner of the depression.
1 80 feet. Climb the corner and then broken rock on the left to a good ledge.
2 30 feet. Climb the steep corner above the belay.

Diamond Crack 90 feet Very Severe (1978*)
The corner/crack between Alouette and the short crack of Solitaire View.
1 90 feet (5a). Climb the crack using the slabby left wall as necessary. Difficulties ease after 60 feet.

The short crack 30 feet right of the wide depression gives a pleasant but slight climb, **Solitaire View** (110 feet, Very Difficult). The short impending crack between this and the easy way down gives the first pitch of **The Exorcist** (70 feet, Hard Very Severe), which then moves left to an easy finish.

Puffins' Parade   220 feet   Very Severe   (1965)
A girdle traverse of the face south of and including the Flying Buttress. Start halfway up the easy way down.
1 70 feet. Meander leftwards over easy rock until it is possible to swing round onto the belay of Alouette.
2 50 feet (4c). Traverse easily left for a few feet and continue with increasing difficulty on holds above the impending wall. Continue left to a flake belay. An intimidating and exposed pitch.
3 60 feet (4c). Move left into the corner formed by the Flying Buttress. Step round onto the buttress and move left to black-streaked rock. Make a descending traverse left (Horseman's Route reversed) across the slab to a belay on the Flying Buttress Route.
4 40 feet. Climb the broken rock above to the top.

The next climb lies on the south-facing cliff directly below the Old Battery and opposite St. Patrick's Buttress. It is approached by descending the long open gully south of the Old Battery, as for Ramrod.

Incantations   140 feet   Very Severe   (1979*)
Start at high tide level immediately right of an obvious dyke.
1 65 feet (4c). Climb up to the overhang, traverse right above a dubious flake and swing round to a good ledge. Nut belays.
2 75 feet (4b). Step up to the left onto a hanging slab and climb it. Continue in the same line on sound holds up the apparently-loose wall to the top.

Just south of the Old Battery is a long open gully. A small steep cliff (OS Ref. 1283 4487) rises out of the right (facing out) wall of the gully about halfway up. The approach is from the south by a steep traverse into the gully about 150 feet above sea level and just below a small wall.

Ramrod   85 feet   Very Severe   (1971)
The wide crack in the centre of the wall, the top pitch is steep and bold for the grade. Start below the crack.
1 45 feet (4c). Climb on good holds to a niche. Pull steeply out of the niche to a large stance beneath the top crack.
2 40 feet (4c). Climb the crack to the top.

West Coast—Quarter Wall to the Old Light

The sea level cliffs on this stretch of coast are divided into two sections by a small promontory halfway, some 250 yards north of the Old Light. This is Sunset Promontory; it presents a steep south face and an overhanging nose to the west, to the north grassy slopes lead down to sea level. To the north of Sunset Promontory is Landing Craft Bay, where the cliff line is broken and there are a number of separate buttresses; to the south there is a virtually unbroken line of sea cliffs terminating in the Old Light Cliff due west of the Old Light. At low tide it is possible to traverse beneath the cliffs from Landing Craft Bay to the Old Light Cliff.

Between the Old Light and the Quarter Wall are a number of small lichen-covered buttresses just below plateau-level similar in nature but not in appearance to the Cheeses. These give a number of pitches but in general the climbing is scrappy and undistinguished.

LANDING CRAFT BAY
This area, which is very close to the camp site etc., provides a fair number of good climbs of medium length at all except the easiest and the hardest grades. Access is reasonable and possible at all states of the tide.

The cliffs in the bay are approached by descending the valley of the stream running down to the sea some 300 yards north of the Old Light. 150 feet above the sea, the valley steepens into a wide area of broken rock and grass immediately north of Sunset Promontory. The descent is then down the steep grassy south side of the next subsidiary gully to the north—it is best to descend the southerly arête of the gully for some distance until a traverse leads to the right (facing out) into the gully. The sea level boulders can also be reached at low tide by a 60-foot abseil from the easy way down to the Flying Buttress.

The smaller buttresses in Landing Craft Bay are named in relation to the former way down described above. Going north from Sunset Promontory, there is first the area of broken rock and grass and then a small slender buttress, First Buttress South, which is followed by the descent gully. Continuing north, there is first a narrow buttress with a black/brown front face containing a number of overhangs; this is First Buttress North. There is then a wide orange rock scar with massive boulders at its foot, which is all that remains of Second Buttress North. Finally there is the distinctive brown cliff, St. Patrick's Buttress, which lies immediately south of the foot of the long open gully of Ramrod.

ST. PATRICK'S BUTTRESS   OS Ref. 1283 4478

This is about 120 yards long with a smooth southerly face made up of alternate slabs and walls slanting up to the right. In contrast, its north westerly face presents a steep wall broken by overhangs, corners and a smooth ledge-line at half height—this face is clearly visible from the Old Battery. The obvious central corner between the two faces is Shamrock.

Evictor   140 feet   Hard Very Severe   (1972/1974)
A steep, spectacular and very sustained route starting up the wide irregular chimney in the overhanging wall left of Shamrock.
1 70 feet (5a/b). Climb the chimney and exit by pulling up to the left and moving up to a glacis. Belay in the bay to the left of the dividing pillar above.
2 70 feet (5b). Climb the groove above via a small groove and crack in the left wall. This pitch can be avoided by the Original Finish, which is as for Shamrock.

Shamrock   160 feet   Hard Severe   (1972/1974)
A good route, now somewhat disjointed in line because of a rock-fall which has made the natural finish considerably harder. Start below the obvious corner.
1 70 feet (4b). Climb the corner, hard to start, until it is possible to traverse left to a nut belay on a large sloping ledge.
2 40 feet (4a). Climb a short crack on the left to gain the large slabby ledge that crosses the left hand face. Belay below the right hand of the two corners above.
3 50 feet (4b). Climb the corner and then easier rock to the top.

Variation   **Direct Finish**   80 feet   Hard Very Severe   (1977)
2a 80 feet (5a). Climb the crack left of the rock scars until it is possible to traverse back into the corner, which leads to the top.

Rampart   120 feet   Hard Very Severe   (1972)
A fine route which takes the narrowing ramp right of Shamrock and then breaks out right to an exposed crack. Start at the foot of Shamrock.
1 40 feet. Cross a slab to the right and move up left to a stance at the foot of the ramp.
2 80 feet (5b). Follow the ramp up to the left with increasing difficulty until a peg in the horizontal crack beneath the overhang can be used to gain holds on the right. Pull round the rib to a crack, which is climbed to the top.

Motorman   200 feet   Hard Very Severe   (1972)
A disjointed route, lacking a decent central pitch but with a spectacular finish up the obvious break at the left end of the upper overhangs on the southerly face. Start to the right of a short crack in the right wall of the spur on the left side of the face.
1 100 feet (4c). Enter the crack by crossing a green slime-streaked slab and climb it to the top of the spur, which is followed to the left end of the terrace. Walk right to a peg belay as for Cow Pie.
2 40 feet. Climb the wall behind the belay and just left of the slanting crack of Destiny to a stance and peg belay.
3 60 feet (5a). Traverse left until beneath the left end of the break in the overhangs and climb directly up to the overhang, peg runner. Climb the overhang using a sling (tape) on a rickety flake for aid above the overhang. Then move up and right then back left to finish.

Destiny   210 feet   E2   (1972)
An excellent route whose second pitch gives sustained and varied jamming, steep and tiring but with superb rock and protection. It takes the conspicuous slanting crack-line in the amphitheatre wall that forms the right hand section of the southerly face. Start directly below the left end of the crack, at a groove in the lower wall.
1 110 feet (4c). Climb the groove and continue up the glacis to the crack, which is climbed for 40 feet to a stance where it narrows.
2 100 feet (5b). Climb the crack, finally gaining a sloping ledge beneath a huge nest. Move right and climb a corner to the top.

Cow Pie   150 feet   Severe   (1972)
A surprisingly easy climb up an impressive area of rock. It takes a diagonal line from right to left across the southerly face, crossing Destiny below the crack of that climb. Start below the obvious weakness in the right side of the lower wall, above and to the right of the groove of Destiny.
1 70 feet. Climb up to the left to gain the glacis and continue leftwards to a peg belay above a small pedestal.
2 80 feet (4a). Climb the wall above trending to a groove, which leads to the top. Peg belays. Scramble off to the right.

Escape Route   220 feet   Very Difficult   (1977*)
Start below the far right side of the southerly face.
1 120 feet. Climb easily to the glacis. Scramble up to the right to the fault line in the right side of the top wall. Poor nut belay.
2 100 feet. Climb the fault line to join Destiny at the ledge below the nest. Move right and climb the corner to the top.

FIRST BUTTRESS NORTH   OS Ref. 1292 4462

Centaur   160 feet   Hard Very Severe   (1972)
A good route with varied and interesting climbing; the crux, which is at the top, is short and well protected. The climb takes the deep V-chimney in the nose of the buttress and finishes up to the right. Start by scrambling up easy rock on the north face to belay where it steepens.
1 60 feet (4a). Climb diagonally right over slabs to belay on nuts at the foot of the chimney.
2 100 feet (5a). Climb the chimney to the roof then move right to a ledge and move up to the big overhang, which is turned by an awkward move to the right round the arête to a small ledge. Peg runner, awkward belay possible. Climb the groove above and then easily up the ramp. Where the ramp steepens make some difficult moves to gain a wide flake crack, which leads to an easy rib. Spike belay (tape).

Road Runner   140 feet   Hard Very Severe   (1972)
This takes the crack in the smooth central face, to the right of the overhanging nose, and then turns the overhang above to the left. The first pitch is excellent and the second not without interest. Start on the jumble of rocks at the foot of the crack line.
1 90 feet (4c). Move up into the crack and follow it to nut belays in the bay below the overhangs.
2 50 feet (5a). Step left and pull steeply up to a peg (in situ). Use the peg to move up to a hidden hold to the left of the overhang. Swing up to the left into a crack, which leads to easy ground—junction with Centaur. Spike belay above.

Scrabble   170 feet   Hard Very Severe   (1972*)
An intricate line with some interesting climbing up the right side of the buttress. Start to the right of the buttress.
1 70 feet (4c). Climb the slab easily and then the first small groove to a black-streaked wall. Avoid this on the right and climb a vague groove to a ledge.
2 35 feet (4c). Step down and traverse left to a corner, which is climbed to a good nut belay in the recess—as for Road Runner.
3 65 feet (5b). Climb the groove above then step round into another groove on the right. Traverse right with difficulty to a small ledge then trend left to a recess. Move right and finish up a groove.

FIRST BUTTRESS SOUTH   OS Ref. 1289 4458

Formula One   130 feet   Hard Very Severe   (1972)
A superb pitch, sustained and varied, which takes the
conspicuous groove in the right wall of the buttress and then
breaks out to the right up steep cracks. Start below the groove.
1 130 feet (5a). Climb a crack to the foot of the groove. Climb
the groove then move right at the roof and up a slanting crack.
Move up and left to a layback-flake, which leads to a short final
corner.

Hot Rod   135 feet   Very Severe   (1977*)
The crack high up in the right wall of the buttress. Start at the
foot of the gully that bounds the buttress to the right.
1 80 feet. Climb the white slabs right of the gully for 30 feet then
move left into the groove, which is followed to a stance beneath
the obvious crack in the left wall.
2 55 feet (4c). Climb the crack to the top.

Gulf Stream   150 feet   Very Severe   (1977)
The brown-coloured slab on the right side of the buttress. A
rather slight climb but interesting in its poorly protected lower
section. Start 20 feet right of the gully that bounds the buttress
to the right.
1 90 feet (4c). Climb broken rock for 25 feet then the slab some
20 feet right of the gully. Step right at the horizontal break then
climb diagonally leftwards to easier ground. Move up to a stance
on the right.
2 60 feet (4a). Step up right then move onto the slab above by a
short leftwards traverse. Climb the crack in the slab and move
left to finish.

SUNSET PROMONTORY   OS Ref. 1287 4449

Various approaches are possible. Perhaps the best, though the
longest and only possible at low tide, is to descend to Landing
Craft Bay and then to traverse back south at sea level round the
foot of the Promontory to the small zawn immediately to its
south. The small zawn can be approached more directly either by
descending the stream as for Landing Craft Bay and then breaking
back to the south above the cliff line or by taking a diagonal line
down from the Old Light to the same point. The descent is then
by a 150-foot abseil down the southerly face of the spur south of
the Promontory (Alpine Buttress) into the small zawn—a few
feet of earthy descent are required to reach the abseil point. A
third method of approach is by abseil down either the south face
or the seaward nose of the Promontory itself, in which case a
short treacherous earthy rib has to be descended to reach the top
of the Promontory (rope useful).

The above mentioned rib is the most direct way off from the top of the Promontory. A more pleasant way off, certainly less frightening, is to go down the grassy north slope of the Promontory to Landing Craft Bay—possible at all tides.

Occidental Groove   120 feet   Hard Severe   (1972)
A short climb whose second pitch gives some interesting climbing up the open-book corner just south of the nose of the Promontory. Start at low tide, to the left of the south face of the Promontory.
1 60 feet (4a). Climb seaweedy rock and then a short steep wall by its right edge to a large flat ledge. Cross the ledge to belay beneath the corner. This point can be approached from the north.
2 60 feet (4b). Make a difficult move up a small groove just right of the m in corner then follow the corner to a flake belay at the top.

Eclipse   130 feet   Hard Severe   (1976/1977)
A magnificent climb on excellent rock in exposed position. Start at half tide, at the foot a short chimney to the left of the prominent arête in the left side of the south face.
1 60 feet (4a). Climb the chimney to an overhang at 15 feet then swing boldly right to the crack in the arête, which is followed to a good ledge.
2 70 feet (4a). Climb up to a large spike on the right side of the arête and climb the slab above to the top.

Variation   Right Hand Start   65 feet   Hard Very Severe   (1976*)
Start beneath the obvious diagonal groove/crack.
1a 65 feet (5a). Climb the groove/crack strenuously until it is possible to pull over to the ramp on the left. Move up to a good stance.

Beam Up   130 feet   Hard Very Severe   (1977*)
An enjoyable pitch up cracks in the steep wall left of Black Hand.
1 60 feet. As for Black Hand.
2 70 feet (5a). Climb diagonally to the left to a spike and continue up the wall, bearing slightly right, to join the arête of Eclipse at the very top.

The Black Hand   135 feet   Very Severe   (1972)
A good climb up the impressive groove with triple overhangs to the right of the undercut buttress of Eclipse, an intimidating pitch for its grade. Start at half tide beneath the groove.
1 60 feet. Climb a chimney and then a wide crack to a large stance.
2 75 feet (4c). Climb the groove to the top.

Garden Rake   130 feet   Severe   (1972*)
The obvious line slanting from left to right across the face right
of The Black Hand. Start below broken rock at the foot of the
rake.
1 100 feet. Climb up to the start of the rake, which is followed
to a belay at an obvious pinnacle where the rake ends.
2 30 feet. Climb the vegetated, broken crack line to the top.
Belay well back on large boulders.

ALPINE BUTTRESS AREA   OS Ref. 1289 4445
Alpine Buttress is the narrow buttress immediately south of
Sunset Promontory. The climbing lies on the south face of the
buttress and in the zawn immediately south of the buttress. The
approach is at low tide as for Sunset Promontory, or by
abseiling directly down the south face of the buttress more or
less from the same point as the abseil to Sunset Promontory.
The latter approach can be used at somewhat higher tides for
routes such as Wolfman Jack. A low tide approach can also be
made from the Old Light Cliff.

Alpine Ridge   150 feet   Very Difficult   (1972)
An enjoyable but loose little ridge climb up the jagged seaward
arête of the buttress. Start at the foot of the arête.
1 70 feet. Follow the slabby face of the arête then climb blocks
on the left side of the arête to a flat section. Traverse along this
to belay below the next steep section in the arête.
2 50 feet. Climb the left wall of the arête to belay beneath the
final small tower.
3 30 feet. Climb the short groove above to the top.

Solomon Grundy   150 feet   Hard Severe   (1979*)
The corner between the walls immediately right of Alpine Ridge.
1 70 feet (4b). Climb up ledges to the crack in the corner. Climb
this keeping right of the ridge until forced onto it. Follow the
ridge for a few feet to a block belay.
2 80 feet. Finish up Alpine Ridge.

Fusion   150 feet   Very Severe   (1977)
The crack high in the wall right of Solomon Grundy. Start on the
ledge below the crack.
1 70 feet (4c). Climb up to the left up a slab towards the corner
of Solomon Grundy then traverse right and make a steep move
up to the foot of the crack, which is climbed to a block belay on
Alpine Ridge.
2 80 feet. Finish easily up Alpine Ridge.

Scorched Earth 160 feet E2 (1977*)
An excellent, technical pitch on impeccable rock up the superb
roofed corner in the south arête of Alpine Buttress. Start at the
sloping ledge at the foot of the corner.
1 140 feet (5c). Climb the corner, passing the first overhang, to a
niche below the next overhang. Climb round this to a little ledge
on the arête below a sentry box. Move up to the final roof and
make a strenuous swing over to a good ledge. Climb a short wall
and belay on good ledges below a steep crack, peg belay.
2 20 feet (4c). Climb the crack to the top.

Moby Dick 220 feet Hard Very Severe (1973)
A good climb up the series of slabby grooves in the right hand
side of the south face of Alpine Buttress. Start at low tide, 20
feet right of a narrow black cave.
1 100 feet (4c). Climb easily up white rock to an overhang at
40 feet, which is climbed awkwardly to good holds above.
Continue up the groove to a sloping stance and peg belay 10
feet below the large roof.
2 70 feet (5a). Cross the slab on the right and climb a groove to a
good ledge. Make some awkward moves into the main groove,
peg runner, and climb this to a stance and peg belay in the left
wall.
3 50 feet (4c). Climb delicately across slabs on the left, peg runner,
to belay on a col in the ridge.

The next two climbs lie in the small zawn immediately south of
Alpine Buttress. Wolfman Jack takes the large steep wall on the
right hand side at the back of the zawn; this is just north of Two
Legged Buttress.

Captain Cat 210 feet E3 (1977*)
A sustained and technical route on excellent rock. The main
pitch takes the crack line in the narrow face to the left of the wall
of Wolfman Jack. Start beneath an obvious wide crack in the
lower wall.
1 80 feet (4c). Climb the crack then easier ground to a block
belay beneath the crack in the narrow face.
2 130 feet (6a). Climb the thin cracks until beneath a smooth
groove. Climb the groove with difficulty and continue up the
wall to sloping ledges. Finish up the groove on the left.

Wolfman Jack 150 feet E2 (1974)
A magnificent, varied climb on perfect rock. It takes the central
crack line in the wall finishing up the obvious square groove.
Start by scrambling up to the right of the foot of the face, up a
black dyke, to some good ledges below a little arête.

1 50 feet (5a). Climb up and step left onto the arête then go left and up the break in the overhang to gain the central crack, which is climbed to a good stance on the left. Peg or nut belay.
2 100 feet (5b/c). Move back right into the crack and climb it to a good ledge, peg runner. Follow the crack and where it splits climb the right hand branch to the overhang. Climb the overhang, peg runner, and the groove above. Good block belays.

Variation   **American Graffiti Finish**   110 feet   E1   (1978*)
2a 110 feet (5b). Climb the crack to the good ledge then take a leftward-rising line for 20 feet to a weakness in the wall. Climb the wall, over three small overlaps, to the top finishing 30 feet left of the parent route.

THE OLD LIGHT AREA
The quality of the climbing in this area and, on the seaward faces, the excellent position more than compensate for the complications of the approach.

Beneath the Old Light, the long line of sea cliffs south of Sunset Promontory and Alpine Buttress terminate in a slabby arête overlooking the long gully that descends due west from the Old Light. The cliff with the slabby arête is the Old Light Cliff.

The approach is down steep ground to the south of the Old Light Cliff. It is best to make a long descending traverse to the south until about 150 feet above the sea and then to traverse steeply back to the north and down grass to sea level. A tedious and at times mildly desperate descent, on which care is required. The seaward faces are then approached at low tide by traversing on sea level boulders. The cliffs can also be approached at low tide from the north and an approach from the abseil south from Alpine Buttress may be preferred for Two Legged Buttress. An increasingly popular approach to the Albacore Slab, on the Old Light Cliff, is to make a 250-foot abseil down that route.

Immediately north of the Old Light Cliff, whose slabby seaward face is formed by the slab of Albacore, is the imposing black wall of Black Crag. Between this and Alpine Buttress is Two Legged Buttress, which is distinguished by a cave/zawn in the middle and a clean slab at the foot of its left leg.

TWO LEGGED BUTTRESS   OS Ref. 1293 4440

Winkle Picker   140 feet   Very Severe   (1976*)
A pleasant little climb up the clean slab and face of the left leg.
1 140 feet (4b). Climb easily up the slab then step left to a recess. Follow the ramp on the right then move round the arête to a

wall split by a crack, which is climbed to a belay on the ridge above. Scramble up the large grassy ramp to the top.

Sexcrime   200 feet   Hard Very Severe   (1976)
A very good route, which should become popular, up the hanging crack and corner between the two legs of the buttress.
1 50 feet (4a). Climb the right edge of the left leg and move right round the arête where it steepens to a nut belay below a steep crack.
2 25 feet (4c). Climb the crack to a good belay ledge.
3 125 feet (4c).   Climb the corner, moving left at the overhang, and belay on the rib.

Chair Ladder   190 feet   Hard Very Severe   (1973*)
Reminiscent of the climbing on its namesake. Start below the left edge of the right leg, at the foot of an ill-defined crack line.
1 60 feet (5a). Climb a rounded groove to reach the crack, which is climbed to a ledge on the right.
2 70 feet (5a). Traverse left for 10 feet to a crack, which is climbed awkwardly past some loose chockstones to a grassy ledge round to the right.
3 60 feet (4c). Climb the crack and groove above the stance and then a diagonal crack to the top.

Pinstripe   160 feet   Severe   (1976*)
Start at low tide on the boulders in the bed of the zawn right of the right leg.
1 80 feet (4a). Climb the crack on the left then go up and left across the slab to belay on the arête.
2 80 feet. Climb the arête on the right then step into the corner, which is followed for 10 feet before moving left to a flake.
Climb twin cracks to a block belay. Scrambling leads to the top.

Bleed for Speed   200 feet   E1   (1976)
A fine, technical route on excellent rock up the left hand of the three impressive grooves in the zawn wall on the right of Two Legged Buttress.
1 120 feet (5c). Climb strenuously through the guarding overhang at 15 feet and step left to the smooth V-groove. Climb the groove to a steep pull through a small overhang then continue up the groove to a hanging nut belay under the large capping roof.
2 80 feet. Move left and climb the corner and then easier ground above to the top. Belay well back.

BLACK CRAG   OS Ref. 1294 4436

Blue Jaunt   220 feet   E3   (1974*)
A difficult and strenuous route in a superb position. It takes a
series of grooves and cracks near the right edge of the wall and
left of Sambo. Start beneath a leftward-slanting crack.
1 100 feet (5a). Climb the crack to pleasant slabs, which lead to
a stance beneath the slanting fault leading into a groove system.
2 120 feet (5c). Climb the fault (as for Sambo) and climb a
smooth arête into the main groove. Climb this for 10 feet then
swing onto the left arête using a downward-pointing spike. Climb
the very steep crack round the rib then continue up cracks to a
square spike. Traverse left and down slightly to a bottomless
groove, which is climbed to the top.

Sambo   240 feet   Very Severe   (1973)
Serious for its grade but pleasant and with open climbing. It
takes the right arête of the black wall. Start on the rounded
boulder in the shallow zawn right of the wall.
1 80 feet (4b). Enter a small sea cave and climb up the back of
the cave until it is possible to gain the obvious crack line.
2 40 feet (4c). Climb the wall above to an obvious black layback
groove, which is climbed to a ledge.
3 30 feet (5a). Climb the diagonal crack round the edge to a
small stance, peg belays.
4 90 feet (4c). The slabby wall above leads pleasantly to the top,
peg runner. Thread belay on blocks at the top.

Variation   50 feet   Hard Very Severe   (1974*)
3a 50 feet (5b). Step right into a groove, which is climbed to the
final wall. Interesting and sustained.

THE OLD LIGHT CLIFF   OS Ref. 1295 4428
Albacore takes the steep slab left (north) of the slabby arête and
Juggernaut takes a crack line up the steep south-facing wall
right of the arête. The top of the buttress, particularly in the area
of the aptly-named Time Bomb, is potentially dangerous ground
due to the seemingly ever-widening fault that separates the
buttress from the mainland.

Lady in White   225 feet   Hard Very Severe   (1978*)
A fine climb up the left side of the Albacore slab. Start at low
tide, below obvious cracks some 30 feet left of the huge boulder
at the foot of Albacore.
1 140 feet (5a). Climb the cracks to gain the left end of a terrace
at 25 feet. Continue up the same crack line to ledges. Move up
and rightwards for a few feet (in common with The Lantern
Man) then take a line up to the left. After 25 feet step left to a

point beneath a bulging shield-like feature. Climb steeply up to gain small ledges. Nut belay to the left. The initial cracks can be avoided if they are wet or inaccessible due to the tide by climbing the first 25 feet of The Lantern Man and then walking along the terrace.

2 85 feet (5a). Climb the crack above the stance and move right where this peters out. Move up and left with difficulty to good finishing holds. Scramble steeply to boulder belays.

The Lantern Man   220 feet   Very Severe   (1978*)
Start just left of the huge boulder at the foot of Albacore.
1 120 feet (4b). Climb to a terrace at 25 feet then go up a thin jagged crack to the right until an upward-traverse can be made to the left to a recess. Move a few feet further left and climb up trending right to a stance and good nut belays.
2 100 feet (4c). Traverse left then move up and back right to the foot of a crack. Climb this until a step left can be made to a small corner and continue to the top. Scramble to block belays (150 feet of rope required).

The original route in this area, **Hunky Dory** (210 feet, Very Severe) takes the line of Lady in White for 80 feet and then follows The Lantern Man to its stance, after which a rightward traverse is followed to join Albacore.

Albacore   190 feet   Hard Very Severe   (1971)
An excellent climb up thin cracks in the seaward-facing slab. Quite easy for its grade but sustained at a reasonable standard. Start on the huge boulder at the foot of the slab—only accessible between half and low tides.
1 140 feet (5a). Step left onto the slab then move up and make an ascending traverse right to the crack line leading up the slab. Climb the crack, passing an overhang where the crack bends to the left, to a stance and peg (thin blades) belay. The peg belay can be avoided by taking a nut belay either below the overhang or above the stance.
2 50 feet (4b). Continue up the crack, which is wider now, to the top. 60 feet of scrambling lead to a good block belay.

Time Bomb   210 feet   E3   (1972)
A first pitch up the slabby arête is followed by a very strenuous and intimidating pitch across the wall on the right.
1 120 feet (4b). Climb easily up to cracks right of the arête and follow these to a stance on the rubble-strewn terrace below the slanting crack in the orange wall.

2 90 feet (5c). Follow the crack to its end. Climb the vertical crack on the right for 5 feet then climb diagonally to the right to gain a hidden ledge at the foot of an overhanging groove, which is climbed to the top.

Juggernaut   200 feet   E1   (1971)
A strenuous route with a bold crux which follows the slightly slanting crack in the south-facing wall. Start below the crack.
1 70 feet (5a). Climb the crack to a pedestal stance. Peg belay.
2 80 feet (5a). Follow the crack line for 20 feet, when it becomes loose, then bear right on good flakes and move up to a horizontal crack. Move back left and climb the wide crack to a stance.
3 50 feet (4c). Climb the corner above, breaking out left at the top.

South West Point

PILOT'S QUAY/GOAT ISLAND AREA

PILOT'S QUAY   OS Ref. 1299 4396

Some 400 yards south of the Old Light, a broken path leads down to a flight of steps that go down the front of the small buttress of Pilot's Quay to sea level. The buttress is detached from the mainland in similar fashion to the Flying Buttress, though much smaller.

A short route is given by the north face of the buttress, **Quay Hole Corner** (60 feet, Very Difficult), which is started by a downwards traverse to a small ledge on the edge of the arch and then follows the left arête of the slabs pleasantly to the top. The broken right hand arête of the front of the buttress gives a rather artificial route, very close to easy rock, **Pacific Portal** (100 feet, Very Difficult), which has some exposure if the edge of the buttress is followed as closely as possible.

ATLANTIC BUTTRESS   OS Ref. 1302 4389

This is the first buttress south (100 yards) of Pilot's Quay. It is approached by descending the rocky rib leading down to the small headland; a traverse is then made to the south until a 20-foot abseil leads down an overhanging groove. The traverse is continued until an obvious fault line slanting up to the right is reached.

Irish Roulette   90 feet   Severe   (1974*)

Start 20 feet left of the slanting fault, below a vertical dyke.

1 40 feet. Climb the dyke for 15 feet and break right onto easier ground. Continue up to a huge belay on perched blocks.

2 50 feet. Step down to the left and traverse back to the dyke. Climb the wall right of the dyke and cross it near the top.

Atlantic Reject   160 feet   Very Severe   (1974*)

Start at the foot of the slanting fault line.

1 60 feet (4c). Follow a rising traverse line up to the right to a niche below an impending corner. Flake belays.

2 40 feet (5a). Climb the corner strenuously to a stance below an overhanging wall left of a black dyke.

3 60 feet. Move left and over the wall on poor rock to gain easier rock then continue straight up. Move back above an overhang and finish up a slab.

CELTIC BUTTRESS   OS Ref. 1313 4380
This is the small buttress on the north side of the headland 50
yards north of Goat Island. A difficult descent is made down the
crest of the headland to sea level; a traverse is then made to the
left (facing in) to the foot of the buttress.

Celtic Shield   250 feet   Very Severe   (1973*)
A good climb, although only on a small face the long traverse on
pitch 2 makes this quite a long climb. Start at low tide at a
slimy groove in the centre of the face.
1 80 feet (4c). Climb the groove to a slab and continue to a stance
on the right below an impressive retaining wall.
2 120 feet (5a). Move left into a grassy groove, which leads onto
the slab above. Climb to the top of the slab and make a long
traverse to the right using the crack under the wall above—two
peg runners near the start. Continue beneath an obvious nose
and past an open corner to a stance and belay.
3 50 feet (4c). Move back to the open corner, which is climbed
passing a loose flake. Continue up a slab to the top.

ROBBIE'S REDOUBT   OS Ref. 1317 4378
This is the small steep cliff immediately north of Goat Island, on
the south side of the Celtic Buttress headland.

Strider   140 feet   Severe   (1974*)
A good route taking an impressive line right of the obvious
fault line.
1 35 feet. Climb up to a small stance beneath a slanting
overhang.
2 65 feet. Climb up to a wide crack in the fault line. Either
climb the crack or the wall on the right (easier) then step left
onto an arête beneath a rightward-slanting groove.
3 40 feet. Climb the groove and then a corner to the top.

MONTAGUE BUTTRESS   OS Ref. 1316 4360
This is the sea level buttress beneath the Montague Steps. The
cliff though small provides some good climbing on large holds up
steep rock. Unfortunately the climbs on the left side are crossed
by a wide ramp. A good place for a quick visit either for an
evening or on a short day.

The approach to the foot of the cliff is from the bottom of the
Montague Steps, from where a traverse to the south is made
along the foot of the cliff on seaweed-covered rocks. This
approach is only possible at lowish tide but a higher traverse can

be made at Very Difficult standard or an abseil(s) can be made from the iron posts at the top of the cliff—in the latter case, it is advisable to take a second rope to reach the cliff edge.

The buttress faces west, is about 120 feet high at its highest and is triangular in shape with its left edge being formed by the slope of the Montague Steps. The top of the buttress is marked by a group of rusty posts from which old cables hang down the face of the buttress. There are two wide rakes slanting up the face to the right. One rake is just below the left edge of the buttress and the other cuts across the centre of the face ending at the point where the cables hang down some 30 feet left of the right edge of the buttress. Cable Way takes the easiest line up the steep rock below the central rake and finishes near the cables.

Cable and Wireless   115 feet   Hard Very Severe   (1970*)
A contrived line which gives some hard technical climbing on its second pitch. Start below a small overhang beneath the mid-point of the central rake, a few feet left of the start of Cable Way.
1 45 feet. Climb the wall to belay on the rake.
2 70 feet. Walk up the rake to the cables. Climb up just left of these for 20 feet (as for Cable Way) then traverse horizontally left with difficulty to a layback-flake, which leads to the top.

Cable Way   110 feet   Very Difficult   (1969)
A good, well-positioned climb. Start at the foot of the most prominent crack slanting up to the right below the central rake.
1 60 feet. Climb the crack for 20 feet, when steep climbing on large holds leads to a niche. Move right and go up to a ledge. Climb straight up, or move right then up and back left, to a broken corner. Climb the corner to a belay on the high point of the central rake.
2 50 feet. Climb steep broken rock just left of the cables to the top. Care with loose rock required.

Sundance   120 feet   Severe   (1971)
A pleasant climb up steep rock on large holds. Start on a slab above the seaweed-level below the right edge of the buttress and to the right of the cables.
1 120 feet. Climb to the top of the slab and up to an overhang. Traverse right under the overhang to a crack. Climb the crack on good holds for 20 feet, when a traverse right across a black wall leads past a dubious block to a groove in the right edge of the buttress. Climb the groove to an overhang, which is turned on the right, then climb up to the left to finish.

WEIRD WALL AREA
There are two large cliffs in the bay south of the Montague Steps. The continuation of Montague Buttress curves round to the south to form a large south-facing cliff that slants up to the right above a steep grass slope. Beneath the grass slope and forming the south side of the bay is Weird Wall, which is characterised by a series of rightward-slanting slabs with steep intervening walls.

The approach to both crags is by descending the grass slope just north of the top of Weird Wall. The top of this slope can be hard to identify and it is best to follow the cliff top closely from the top of Weird Wall—even so a few feet of very exposed ground have to be crossed. An alternative approach, which avoids the potential dangers of the direct approach, is at low-tide from the foot of the Montague Steps.

MONTAGUE WALL   OS Ref. 1324 4359
The south side of the Montague Steps promontory is a big yellow wall, which looks most unstable. The rock is in fact reasonable once gardened.

Verdict   230 feet   Hard Very Severe   (1975*)
A good route with impressively steep climbing on the first pitch and fine positions above. The rock is friable in places but sound enough generally. The route starts up the narrow dyke some 50 feet left of the wide basalt dyke taken by Queen's Gambit.
1 100 feet (5a). Follow the dyke crack over several overhangs until beneath a large roof split by a wide crack, peg runner in place. Move into the crack above the overhang from the right and climb to easier ground leading to a small stance, peg and nut belays.
2 80 feet (4b). Take the obvious line rightwards to a groove on the crest of the buttress. Climb this then move up left to another groove, which leads to a large sloping stance. Peg belays.
3 50 feet (4b). Climb the buttress above on good holds to a groove, which leads to the boulder slope above.

The Queen's Gambit   205 feet   Hard Very Severe   (1974*)
The climb is centred on the large basalt dyke left of the centre of the face. Start 30 feet right of the dyke.
1 35 feet (4b). Climb a steep slab to a ledge and nut belays below the large roof.
2 50 feet (5b). Traverse left and step across the dyke. Climb up beside it for 20 feet to a slabby scoop, peg runner. Make a very hard move across the steep wall on the right to regain the dyke. Peg belay in the chimney above.

3 80 feet (4c). Continue up the dyke until the angle eases and it is possible to gain the steep slab on the right. Climb this and trend to the right (almost on Montague Python). Move up and left and belay at the foot of a short overhanging corner.
4 40 feet (4b). Climb the corner then loose rock above to the top. Belay well back.

Montague Python 190 feet   Hard Very Severe (1974)
A good climb taking a direct line up the centre of the face and finishing up the prominent roof crack. Start at the foot of the obvious small groove where the gully at the foot of the face steepens and becomes rocky at the bottom, some 60 feet right of the wide basalt dyke of The Queen's Gambit.
1 20 feet (5a). Climb the groove to a restricted stance.
2 110 feet (4b). Traverse left for 15 feet to a flake. Climb a groove to a stance under the prominent overhang.
3 60 feet (5a). Climb the overhang by the obvious crack to easy but loose ground. Poor belay on a small boulder.

The Good Ship Lollipop 190 feet   Hard Very Severe (1974*)
Start as for Montague Python.
1 130 feet (5a). Climb the starting groove of that climb then continue straight up to the left of the slab. Gain the slab and traverse right for a few feet until beneath a bulge at the foot of a groove. Climb this direct until a stance can be taken a few feet right of the stance of Montague Python.
2 60 feet (5a). Climb the steep groove above until a steep slab beneath the roof is reached. Traverse left and make an awkward swing round the arête to a groove, which is climbed to the top. Belays well back.

Hooka 140 feet   Very Severe (1974*)
Start on the pillar a few feet right of Montague Python.
1 80 feet (4c). Climb up to a slab slanting right. Traverse right on the slab, awkward, and continue straight up the groove at the end of the traverse then over loose blocks to a ledge and good block belay.
2 60 feet (4c). Make a short traverse across the steep wall on the right to a groove, which is followed over a dubious block to a good spike. Traverse right along an obvious line for 10 feet then climb to the top.

Sunblest   120 feet   Severe   (1974*)
The obvious depression right of Hooka.
1 60 feet. Climb the corner and good slabs then enter the groove
from the left and climb to a large ledge with good belays.
2 60 feet. Regain the groove and continue to the top.

WEIRD WALL   OS Ref. 1328 4352
A large and, as the name implies, rather strange cliff which
gives interesting and very varied climbing with a long,
complicated and quite exciting approach.

The grass slope above and left of the cliff leads down to a rocky
slope that is crossed by a basalt dyke. Cross the dyke to the
summit of a small south-facing buttress. The approach now
involves some Hard Severe standard climbing for which roping-
up may be preferred. Climb down the face of the small buttress
for 20 feet then traverse back right towards the main cliff and
recross the dyke to gain an amorphous, juggy wall. Pick a route
down to the right to the foot of the wall; Wodwo and the climbs
to its right are approached at lowish tide by jumping a gap to
slabby rock beneath the big wall.

The first two climbs, which share a common first pitch, are
approached at any state of the tide by working up to the right on
the wall after crossing the dyke to a square jutting ledge at the
left hand side of the steep slab above the huge sea cave; belay on
pegs or nuts.

Umbgozi   260 feet   E2   (1975)
This takes a line in spectacular position up slabs above the cave
in the left hand section of the cliff.
1 120 feet (5a). Traverse right across the slab and over to its
right edge, ring peg in place above. Make a difficult swing round
the overhanging arête on the right (loose) to gain the bottom of
another slab. Climb the slab to where it vanishes and cross the
steep wall to gain the continuation slab. Move up to a grassy
ledge and good nut belays.
2 100 feet (5a). Climb the slab above for 20 feet then climb a
crack in the left wall. Continue up the face above to gain a high
steep slab, which is climbed via its corner crack until near its top.
Peg belay in place.
3 40 feet (5a). Continue up the slab and finish up a loose wall.

Mirage Oasis   300 feet   E2   (1976)
This takes the impressive white slab between Umbgozi and Wodwo.
1 120 feet (5a). As for Umbgozi.
2 80 feet (4a). Climb pleasantly up the corner of the slab to nut belays at the top of the slab and beneath the headwall.
3 100 feet (5b). Climb the groove to a narrow ramp leading out right. Climb the ramp to a steep and exposed groove, which leads to the top on fragile holds. Scramble to belays.

Wodwo   270 feet   Hard Very Severe   (1972)
An unusual route, sustained in quality but not in difficulty. The main feature of the wall is a black slabby groove in the upper half above the obvious wide slab. Start some 30 feet right of the gap that is jumped, beneath a short, jutting groove.
1 130 feet (4b). Climb the groove awkwardly to gain the wide slab. Climb the left corner of the slab to easy rock, which leads to a stance and nut belays below a steep flake crack leading to the groove.
2 140 feet (5a). Enter the crack from the right by some hard moves and climb it to gain the first slab. The crack can be approached direct, harder. Continue, past an impressive rock tooth, to a steep layback crack, which leads to the long final slab. Climb the slab then break out left up its retaining wall to a narrow grassy ledge, peg belays. Move left and scramble to the top.

Apsara   280 feet   Hard Severe   (1975)   5/9/83   + Bill T., PS T.E.
A very good climb which combined with the approach gives the spirit of a big route on a serious cliff without the attendant difficulties. It follows the long slab taken by the first pitch of Wodwo in its entirety. Start on the slabby ledges as for Wodwo.
1 140 feet. Traverse right from the ledges to gain a wide crack, which leads up to the left to gain the large slab. Follow the slab easily to a peg belay at a detached flake halfway up the pasture.
2 140 feet (4a). Climb the slab to the top, mostly near its right edge. Thread belays well back.

The next two climbs are approached from the slabby rock after the gap by making a 150-foot traverse along the foot of the cliff at Hard Severe standard to a black slab seamed with cracks. This point could also be approached, wetly, by wading through one of the tunnels north of the Shutter Rock area.

Astral Traveller   200 feet   E3   (1977*)
A very fine, direct route with a sustained top pitch up the wall
left of Wodwo. Start at a belay 10 feet left of the black slab.
1 80 feet (5b). Climb up to gain a sloping ledge beneath a short
corner. Move up the corner then follow a thin crack diagonally
right until holds on the wall above are reached. Move left and
then up to the slab of Wodwo and climb this easily to the belay
of that climb.
2 120 feet (5c). Climb Wodwo for 6 feet then move left and climb
the obvious flake crack, stepping left at its top into a groove.
Move up to the overhang then climb rightwards across the
pocketed wall and pull over an overhang to gain a shallow
groove, which leads to a spike on Mirage Oasis. Traverse right
for 6 feet and climb the wall direct on widely-spaced holds.
Finish with care as for Mirage Oasis and belay well back.

Navigator   200 feet   E1   (1973)
An excellent, varied route which takes the wide impending crack
rising out of the cave at the right side of the wall and then the
intricate slabs and walls above. Start near the top of the black
slab.
1 90 feet (5b). Make a rising traverse into the crack and climb it
to a small stance where it gives over to a slab. Peg belays.
2 50 feet (5b). Climb the wall above the stance to a larger slab
and climb to the overhang at the top of the slab, peg runner.
Using the overhang, traverse right to the arête and climb to a
stance on the big final slab, peg belays.
3 60 feet (4b). Climb the slab and a bulge to the cliff top.
Scramble to belays.

SHUTTER POINT AREA
The cliffs in this area are most impressive and are amongst the
biggest on the island; the rock is better than it looks. In fact, on
Focal Buttress the worst rock is on the ledges, which tend to
consist of masses of unstable boulders, the rock in between
varying from relatively to very sound. The sheer lower left hand
section of Focal Buttress gives a concentration of fine hard
routes with stunning lines. The Devil's Limekiln is in a class of its
own and deserves a visit from anyone who enjoys exploring sea
cliffs.

The approach to Great Shutter Rock and to the cliffs opposite is
by descending a steep grassy spur south of the Devil's Limekiln
until about 150 feet above the sea. Then scramble down across a
steep, but well marked, rocky slope to the north. A rough path
then leads across mixed ground to the spur of earth and rock

that runs out to Great Shutter Rock. The entrance to the Limekiln and the surrounding cliffs can be approached at low tide down boulders to the north of the spur. Ulysses Factor and the climbs to its right can be started at any state of the tide.

The large cliffs opposite Shutter Rock are split in the centre by a chasm leading back to the tall narrow tunnel entrance to the Devil's Limekiln. To the right of this chasm and immediately opposite Shutter Rock is Focal Buttress. To the left are a series of diagonal fault lines and then on the far left a large leaning buttress separated from the main cliff by a steep gully with a jammed boulder near its top. The leaning buttress is the southern headland of the Weird Wall cove.

The next two climbs lie to the north of the large leaning buttress and are just south of Weird Wall. They are approached at dead low tide by wading and then climbing through the cave/tunnel beneath the gully separating the leaning buttress from the mainland. They could also be approached by another tunnel some 30 feet inland, which leads off due north from the entrance to the Limekiln.

Pony and Trap   160 feet   Severe   (1971*)
As the name implies, a climb of dubious quality but set in dramatic surroundings. It takes the nearest slab on the landward side of the cave/tunnel.
1 50 feet. Climb the slab above the water to a ledge.
2 30 feet. Climb up behind the jammed boulder at the top of the gully to the point where the buttress contacts the main cliff.
3 80 feet. Traverse diagonally left on doubtful rock to the skyline. Belay some 30 feet above.

Muffin the Mule   270 feet   Severe   (1977*)
An interesting expedition up the north face of the leaning buttress. Gain the foot of the face by lasso and a tyrolean onto low ledges on the other side of the cleft.
1 70 feet. Climb the right edge of the slab to a poor stance but good nut belay under the big overhang.
2 80 feet (4a). Traverse left to a crack leading up from the left edge of the overhang and follow it to a recess in the slab above. Traverse horizontally into the cleft and belay on the large boulder as for Pony and Trap.
3 120 feet. Climb the gully to the gap and continue up the grassy wall going diagonally left to easier ground.

Ember Wall   250 feet   Hard Severe   (1966)
The steep wall right of the gully with the jammed boulder, on
the south side of the leaning buttress. The top pitch is quite
loose. Start at the foot of the rib leading up to the wall from the
right.
1 60 feet. Gain the rib by climbing a few feet up the chimney on
its right and follow it until it steepens.
2 40 feet. Move round the arête on the left and climb up to a
flake belay on a ledge about 15 feet right of the jammed boulder.
3 150 feet. Various lines are possible up the steep wall above.
Near the top, traverse either left or right to get off the face—the
latter enables a stance to be taken at 100 feet.

THE DEVIL'S LIMEKILN   OS Ref. 1338 4349

The Kiln   340 feet   Very Severe   (1970)
The original ascent of the Devil's Limekiln. It is a matter of
personal taste as to whether the dramatic and unusual setting
compensates sufficiently for the somewhat indifferent climbing.
The climbing is not hard but it is a serious route and the initial
chimney is often wet. It may be worth pre-placing the belay at
the top of the climb. Start by entering the limekiln at low tide
and then by climbing up the mud slope at the back to the
eastern end of the floor of the Limekiln—sheltered stance
recommended.
1 90 feet (4a). Climb the first chimney in the left (north) wall,
two peg runners, then move right to climb the continuation gully.
Peg belay.
2 75 feet. Continue up the chimney above to a prominent loose
flake then traverse left across mixed ground to the foot of the
obvious slab. Peg belay.
3 100 feet (4a). Climb the slab, at first by the corner on its right
and then by trending left along the obvious line. Climb up to a
grassy bulge, which is climbed to a peg belay in a small corner.
4 75 feet (4b). Follow the obvious line up to the left, peg runner,
to finish. Long/ice pegs needed for the belay.

Flashing into the Dark   220 feet   Hard Very Severe   (1977*)
An enjoyable route in its way which epitomises hole in the ground
climbing. It follows the impressive chimney line in the south east
corner of the Limekiln.
1 150 feet (5a). Grovel up the chimney to the grass field, four
peg runners. Belay on a thread in the corner and a large nut to
the right (not obvious).
2 70 feet. Move to the right end of the field, peg runner, then
climb suspect rock for 10 feet and bear left to the top. Stake
belay in place.

The Exorcist   180 feet   E2   (1976)

A tremendous and unusual wall climb starting 150 feet above the floor of the Limekiln. It takes an intricate line up the undercut blank wall in the south side of the Limekiln. The approach is by a 170-foot abseil down the basalt rib left of the wall to a very exposed stance in the loose chimney by the foot of the wall, bong belay. It may be a good idea to keep the abseil rope in place to reinforce the belay, even if this does detract from the purity of the climb.

1 70 feet (5b). Gain the bending crack on the right by some hard moves, peg runner. Follow the crack to where it peters out at an overlap, peg runner in place. Traverse delicately left under the overhang until it is possible to cross it to gain a small stance beneath a crescent-shaped overhang. Large nut and blade peg belay.

2 110 feet (5a). Step left to a line of good holds, which lead to a smooth scoop, peg runner. Follow a shallow rib up to the right to a horizontal fault, peg runner in place. Step left and follow a shallow depression to a small ledge. Move up left for 15 feet then move right to a small overlap, go over this and climb straight to the top. Peg belays.

FOCAL BUTTRESS   OS Ref. 1338 4343

This is the large conical buttress immediately opposite Shutter Rock. The foot of the buttress is formed by the scree slope that runs down to the entrance of the Limekiln. The lower left hand section is an impressive steep wall, some 150 feet high, above which the buttress falls back in a series of large broken ledges and short steep walls. The lower wall is split near its top by the prominent black groove of Ulysses Factor; another feature is the long narrow ledge of that climb near the foot of the wall. To the right the angle eases and there is a line of broken cracks leading up to the lichen-covered tower that forms the summit of the buttress.

The next two climbs share a common low tide start and pegs should not be used as the crack is almost worn out already.

The Great Divide   340 feet   E2   (1977)

A route of outstanding character giving sustained jamming in an unrelentingly steep situation. It takes the soaring crack in the impending wall that forms the left side of Focal Buttress, just right of the entrance to the Limekiln. Start just right of the smooth base of the arête.

1 140 feet (5b). Use combined tactics to place a very small wire nut and use it to reach holds by a good thread, which is used for resting. Climb the thin crack just left of the arête to better holds where it darts left for 5 feet. Continue up the crack to a peg belay where it finally gives out onto a short slab. Large nuts needed for runners.

2 100 feet (4b). Move left and go up the slab into the corner on the left. Take the easiest line up this to a large ledge and pointed block belay below the final wall.

3 100 feet (4c). As for Wild Country, step left off the block and climb the wall to a crack, which leads right to easy slabs.

Golden Gate   320 feet   E3   (1977*)

A very sustained route of the highest calibre which takes the left arête of Focal Buttress and then the narrow face set above the entrance to the Limekiln. Start just right of the base of the arête.

1 150 feet (5c). Use combined tactics and then a small wire nut to reach holds above, good thread. Climb steeply up the right side of the arête for 15 feet then step right to good holds, which lead to a ledge. Follow the arête using the thin crack to another ledge then continue up the true arête (the crack on the right is Wild Country) to reach the easier-angled rib above. Climb to a good nut belay in a cracked slab beneath an overhang.

2 100 feet (5b). Make a rising traverse left to a corner containing large blocks. Climb up until level with a tall pointed block, after about 15 feet, then move onto the wall on the left. Continue diagonally to the left and just before the edge of the wall climb up to a stance. Good nut belays.

3 70 feet (5b). Climb easily up the ramp above the stance for 15 feet then enter the overhanging groove that overlooks the ramp and climb it awkwardly to easier terrain. Belays well back.

Wild Country   340 feet   E3   (1974*)

A superb route which climbs the face just right of the arête of Golden Gate. Start about 15 feet right of the arête, on a huge green boulder.

1 90 feet (5c). Use combined tactics to place a poor peg, which is used for aid to place another poor aid peg. Climb diagonally left with difficulty to a small ledge. Climb up bearing slightly to the right then directly on excellent holds to a point where the wall starts impending below an enticing flake. Climb steeply up to the flake. Stance and large nut belays.

2 80 feet (4c). Climb the rib above and then slabby rock to belay beneath a short corner.

3 70 feet (4b). Climb the corner then continue easily over ledges to belay on a large pointed block beneath the final wall.

4 100 feet (4c). Step left off the block and climb the wall to a crack, which leads rightwards to easier finishing slabs.

Olympica 300 feet E4 (1977*)
The hardest route on the island taking an incredible-looking line up the wall between Wild Country and Ulysses Factor. Start about 35 feet right of the left arête, at a vague line of weakness.
1 150 feet (6a). Climb up for 10 feet then move left to better holds and go diagonally left to a point about 15 feet right of and slightly lower than the enticing flake of Wild Country. Climb diagonally right across the steep featureless wall for 25 feet then ascend more directly to the top of the face. Nut belays beneath an overhang as for The Great Divide and Golden Gate.
2 150 feet (5a). Climb directly up various walls to the top.

Ulysses Factor 340 feet Very Severe (1970)   *7/9/8? + BᴜᴜT, +Ps*
A very good climb, long and varied with a delightful top pitch. There is still some loose rock but with care this should not be much of a problem. The first pitch can be quite intimidating but once embarked on it proves reasonable. Start some 30 yards up the scree slope, to the right of the long narrow ledge.
1 30 feet (4b). Traverse up to the left along flakes to the ledge. Peg belay.
2 120 feet (4b). Climb up from the right end of the ledge to a traverse line, which leads up to the left to a crack. Follow the crack into the prominent black groove and climb this until a move left can be made onto wide ledges. Peg belay.
3 50 feet. Climb a jagged crack on the right in the short wall above and continue over broken ground to a peg belay below a wall.
4 50 feet (4b). Move down a few feet to the right and climb steeply up the yellow wall trending right to ledges below the final tower. Move right to good nut belays beneath the shallow depression in the lichen-covered summit tower.
5 90 feet (4c). Climb up to the depression and follow it moving left near the top.

Lucifer 300 feet Very Severe (1971*)
This takes the wall right of Ulysses Factor and then crosses Focal Face to finish up the right side of the summit tower.
1 30 feet. As for Ulysses Factor.
2 70 feet. Follow Ulysses Factor for a few feet then continue directly up the centre of the face on sound rock, moving right to a ledge belay.
3 30 feet. Move left from the corner and then climb the face diagonally to the left to the obvious horizontal fault. Peg belay.
4 70 feet. Traverse right, crossing Focal Face, and climb a white slab to a small stance and peg belays in a horizontal crack.
5 100 feet. Climb the obvious rake then climb onto the face above after 50 feet to a stance in a small corner. Belay well back.

Focal Face   260 feet   Very Severe   (1970)
The top pitch is excellent but is also taken by Ulysses Factor,
which otherwise overshadows this route. Start about 35 yards up
the scree slope, some 10 yards right of the narrow ledge of
Ulysses Factor and below a short vertical step in the gully.
1 130 feet (4a). Climb up and left to a shallow groove just left
of some black streaks. Climb the groove and easier rock above.
Keeping left of the obvious crack line continue to a ledge sloping
up to the left and on to a prominent niche above the ledge. Good
nut belays.
2 40 feet. Climb up to the right and out of the niche then
continue over broken ground to the left to good nut belays below
the summit tower.
3 90 feet (4c). Climb the shallow depression in the tower to the
top.

Messin' With The Kid   140 feet   E1   (1975*)
After a scruffy start it takes an impressive thin crack in the right
wall of the lichen-covered summit tower. Small wire runners are
required for protection. Start about 20 feet down the slope at
the foot of the face, where broken turf ledges lead out onto the
face. Move along these (rope advised) to poor belays below a
groove.
1 60 feet (4c). Climb the groove until it ends at a ramp. Move up
this to the right for 10 feet to a nut and peg belay.
2 80 feet (5b). Move up to the thin crack in the wall above and
climb it until good holds on the right gain the top. A spike at
60 feet should not be used too vigorously. A very sustained pitch.

GREAT SHUTTER ROCK AREA
When seen from inland, Great Shutter Rock presents a steep
triangular face with an earthy rib connecting it to the mainland.
This face is very unstable and appears to be continuously falling
to bits, so much so that a route up the right hand side has
disappeared. The remaining route traverses out to the left from
the shoulder and then goes up to the left hand ridge on crumbling
layback edges (30 feet, Severe, 1963*).

The next climb lies in the first major zawn (OS Ref. 1344 4338)
west of the zawn south of the col above the foot of Focal
Buttress. It is approached by going along the path to Great
Shutter Rock until the grass slope on the left can be ascended to
gain the ridge above the path. The long ridge leading down to a
prominent rock island is then descended until a lowish tide
traverse can be made into the back of the zawn east of the
ridge.

The Minatour   220 feet   Hard Very Severe   (1977*)
The zawn goes back some way into the hillside with a huge
jammed boulder at the back. The climb takes the slab on the
left to reach the overhang and then traverses right above the lip
of the overhang in fine position.
1 30 feet. Climb the rightward-leading line of holds to gain the
top of the wedged boulder at the back of the zawn.
2 90 feet (4c). Traverse left on the slab for 40 feet then go up the
middle of the slab to the overhang. Climb to a good stance.
3 50 feet (5a). Step down to the right and cross the slab on the
right then move up into the overhung groove, swing right out of
the groove and go up to a belay.
4 50 feet. Climb the chimney to the top. Belay well back.

HIDDEN ZAWN   OS Ref. 1346 4344
This is the zawn immediately south of the Limekiln. From the
tunnel leading into the Limekiln, another tunnel leads off to the
south east and emerges on the South Coast in Hidden Zawn. A
more straightforward but less adventurous approach is by making
a scrambling descent down the rib bounding the zawn to the west;
this rib is the continuation of the spur that leads down to the
south from the Limekiln. The rib leads to ledges on the west side
of the zawn—the boulders at the foot of the zawn are only
accessible at low tide.

Labyrinth   220 feet   Very Severe   (1976*)
The climb follows the diagonal ramp that splits the west wall of
the zawn. Start on the largest boulder in the zawnbed.
1 20 feet (4b). Climb flakes on the left to a ledge. Chockstone
belay.
2 80 feet (4c). From the right end of the ledge follow the ramp
up to the right until it is possible to step up left to a ledge. Nut
belay.
3 120 feet (4b). Continue rightwards up another ramp to an
overlap, which is climbed to gain the slab above. Climb the slab,
passing another overlap, to the top. Scramble to block belays on
the path.

The Bow   140 feet   Hard Very Severe   (1970*)
A rightward-slanting line up the east wall of the zawn. Start at
the foot of a steep black wall left of a huge black overhang, just
outside the tunnel exit.
1 100 feet. Climb the wall, slippery at first, on small holds and
continue up left into the corner. Higher up, where the angle
steepens, follow a curving line back up to the right on sloping

holds beneath overhanging rock. Using a peg (in place) for aid
step round the arête to a small stance with a nut belay.
2 40 feet. Step down a few feet and traverse round the arête.
Continue round the next arête and then easily to the top.

KISTVAEN BUTTRESS OS Ref. 1352 4339

A small cliff of excellent rock which provides some pleasant
climbing of a go-anywhere nature, this sea level buttress is
situated on the west flank of the first headland east of the
Limekiln and is clearly visible from the spur that is used to
approach the Shutter Point area. The approach is by scrambling
more or less directly down the ridge halfway between the
Limekiln and the Rocket Pole. This leads down to the headland
and the buttress is then just to the west.

The buttress is about 100 feet high and the climber can virtually
wander at will. However, there are four named climbs on the
slabby face left of the easy way down: Justine (100 feet, Very
Difficult) takes the corners immediately left of the way down
finishing up the tower above. **Mount Olive** (100 feet, Very
Difficult) starts up the obvious curving groove in the centre of the
face, moving left after 40 feet. **Clea** (80 feet, Hard Severe) after
starting up the latter takes the overlapping slabs between it and
the former. The slab left of Mount Olive gives **Bitter Lemons**
(110 feet, Severe), which takes a line up to the left.

The face further left is approached by **The Dark Labyrinth** (90
feet, Severe), after a 30-foot traverse left from the ledge below the
previous climbs a move is made up to a continuation traverse
beneath an overhang, which leads to a stance on a steep slab.
Balthazar (100 feet, Very Difficult) goes up this slab for a few
feet and then left to a line up slabs, which leads to the top.

LUNDY

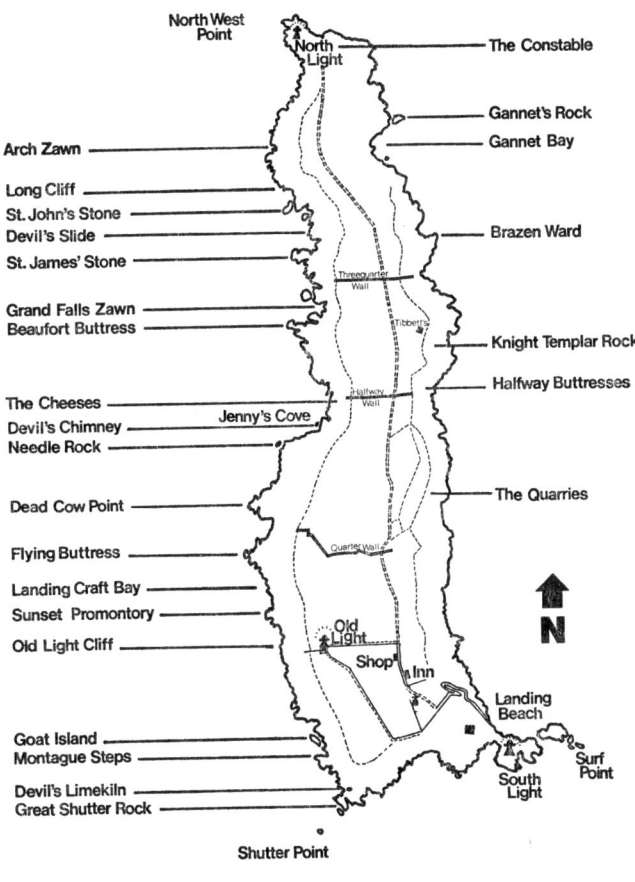

North West Point

North Light

The Constable

Gannet's Rock

Gannet Bay

Arch Zawn

Long Cliff

St. John's Stone

Devil's Slide

St. James' Stone

Brazen Ward

Threequarter Wall

Grand Falls Zawn

Beaufort Buttress

Tibbett's

Knight Templar Rock

Halfway Buttresses

Halfway Wall

The Cheeses

Devil's Chimney

Needle Rock

Jenny's Cove

Dead Cow Point

The Quarries

Flying Buttress

Quarter Wall

Landing Craft Bay

Sunset Promontory

Old Light Cliff

Old Light

Shop

Inn

Landing Beach

N

Goat Island

Montague Steps

Devil's Limekiln

Great Shutter Rock

South Light

Surf Point

Shutter Point

BRGJ '79

0   1

Miles

WEST COAST
Northern Section

N

North West Point

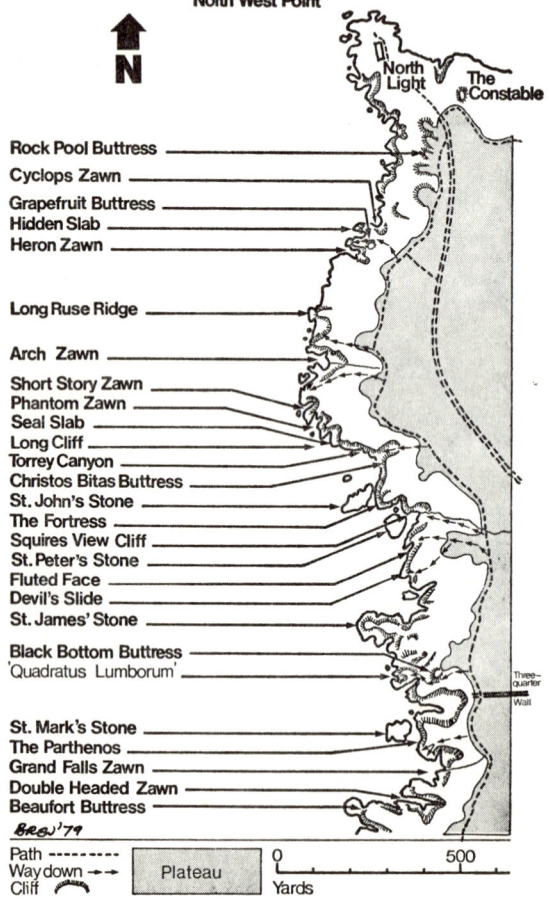

North Light

The Constable

Rock Pool Buttress
Cyclops Zawn
Grapefruit Buttress
Hidden Slab
Heron Zawn

Long Ruse Ridge

Arch Zawn

Short Story Zawn
Phantom Zawn
Seal Slab
Long Cliff
Torrey Canyon
Christos Bitas Buttress
St. John's Stone
The Fortress
Squires View Cliff
St. Peter's Stone
Fluted Face
Devil's Slide
St. James' Stone

Black Bottom Buttress
'Quadratus Lumborum'

St. Mark's Stone
The Parthenos
Grand Falls Zawn
Double Headed Zawn
Beaufort Buttress

Three-quarter Wall

BREW '79

Path --------
Way down ➡➡
Cliff ⌒

Plateau

0   500

Yards

WEST COAST
Central Section

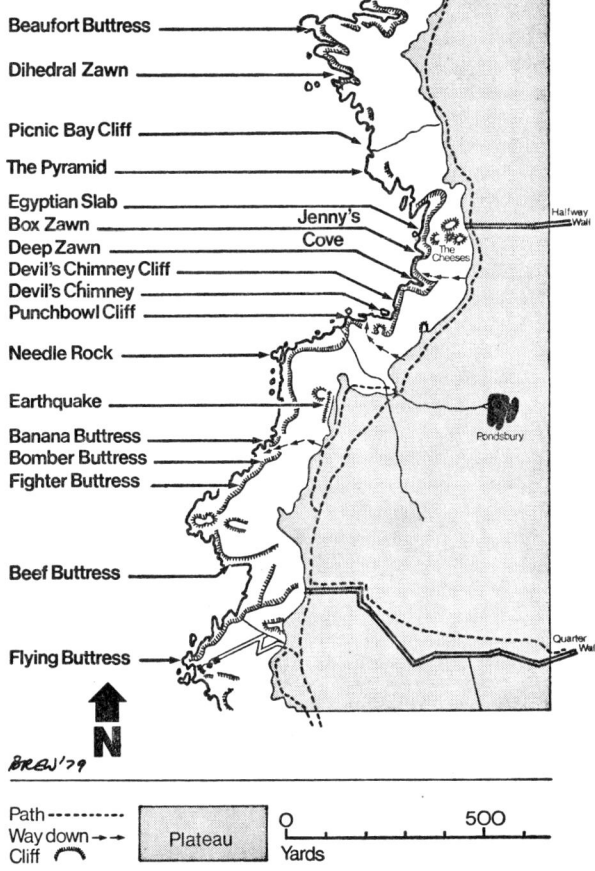

Beaufort Buttress

Dihedral Zawn

Picnic Bay Cliff

The Pyramid

Egyptian Slab

Box Zawn

Deep Zawn

Devil's Chimney Cliff

Devil's Chimney

Punchbowl Cliff

Needle Rock

Earthquake

Banana Buttress

Bomber Buttress

Fighter Buttress

Beef Buttress

Flying Buttress

Jenny's Cove

The Cheeses

Halfway Wall

Pondsbury

Quarter Wall

BREW'79

N

Path - - - - - - - -
Way down → →
Cliff ⌒

Plateau

0   500
Yards

WEST COAST
Southern Section

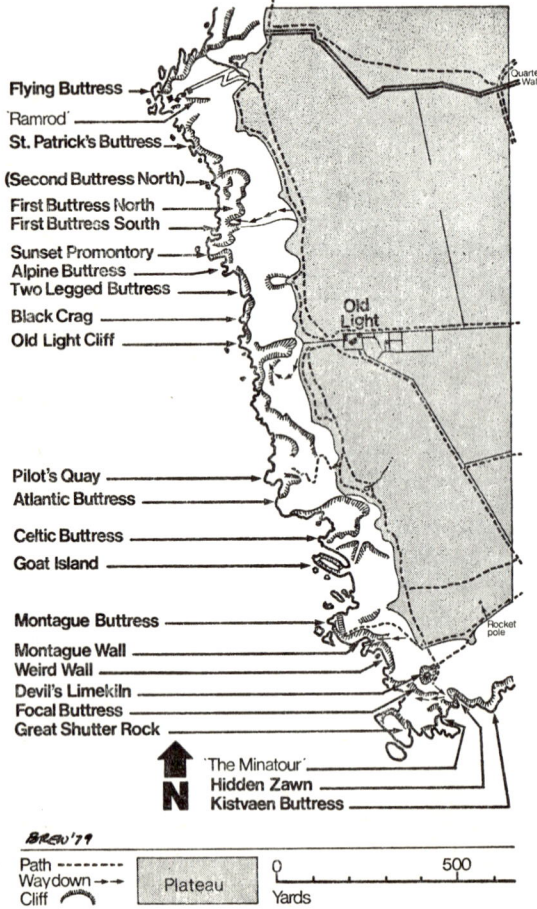

Flying Buttress →

'Ramrod'

St. Patrick's Buttress →

(Second Buttress North) →

First Buttress North
First Buttress South

Sunset Promontory →
Alpine Buttress →
Two Legged Buttress →

Black Crag →

Old Light Cliff →

Old Light

Pilot's Quay →
Atlantic Buttress →

Celtic Buttress →

Goat Island →

Montague Buttress →

Montague Wall →
Weird Wall →
Devil's Limekiln →
Focal Buttress →
Great Shutter Rock →

Quarter Wall

Rocket pole

'The Minatour'
Hidden Zawn
Kistvaen Buttress →

N

BREW '79

Path	--------
Waydown	→→
Cliff	

Plateau

0   500

Yards

ARCH ZAWN

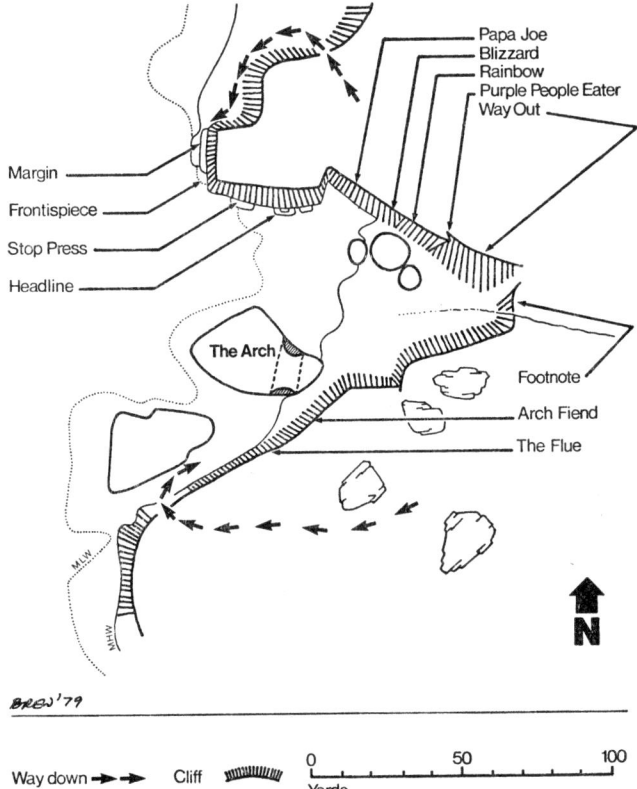

Papa Joe
Blizzard
Rainbow
Purple People Eater
Way Out

Margin
Frontispiece
Stop Press
Headline

The Arch

Footnote

Arch Fiend

The Flue

N

BREW '79

Way down ➤ ➤   Cliff 🗻   0   50   100
Yards

DEVIL'S SLIDE AREA

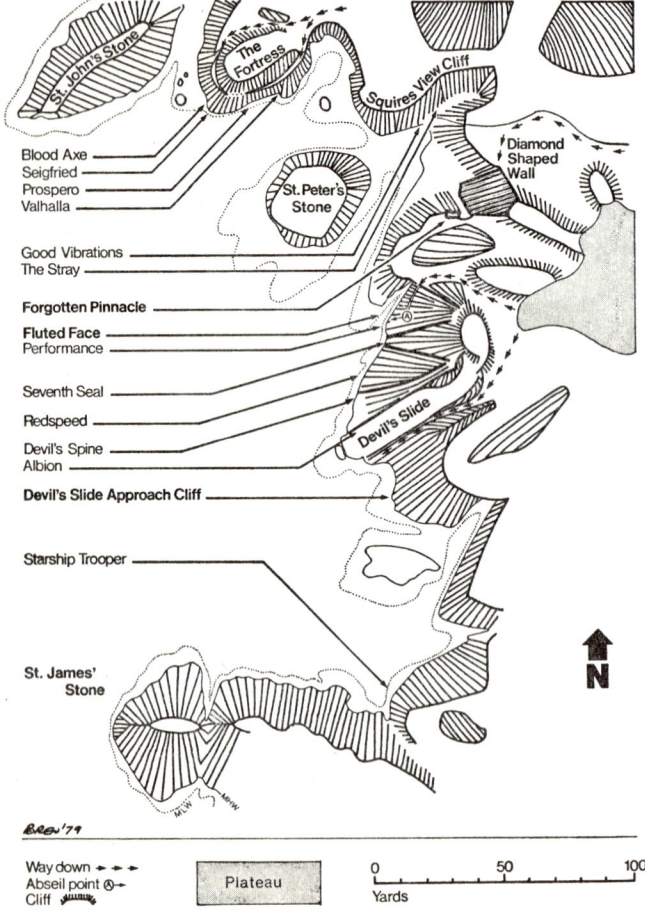

St. John's Stone

The Fortress

Squires View Cliff

Diamond Shaped Wall

Blood Axe
Seigfried
Prospero
Valhalla

St. Peter's Stone

Good Vibrations
The Stray

Forgotten Pinnacle

Fluted Face
Performance

Seventh Seal

Redspeed

Devil's Spine
Albion

Devil's Slide

Devil's Slide Approach Cliff

Starship Trooper

St. James' Stone

BREW '79

Way down ➤ ➤ ➤
Abseil point Ⓐ→
Cliff

Plateau

0   50   100
Yards

N

THE DEVIL'S SLIDE AREA

1 Tempest
2 Performance
3 Magic Flute
4 Sandpiper
5 Magnificat
6 Seventh Seal
7 Redspeed
8 Dexter
9 Devil's Honeymoon
10 Devil's Spine
11 Shark
12 Albion
13 The Devil's Slide

JENNY'S COVE

DEEP ZAWN – DEVIL'S CHIMNEY AREA

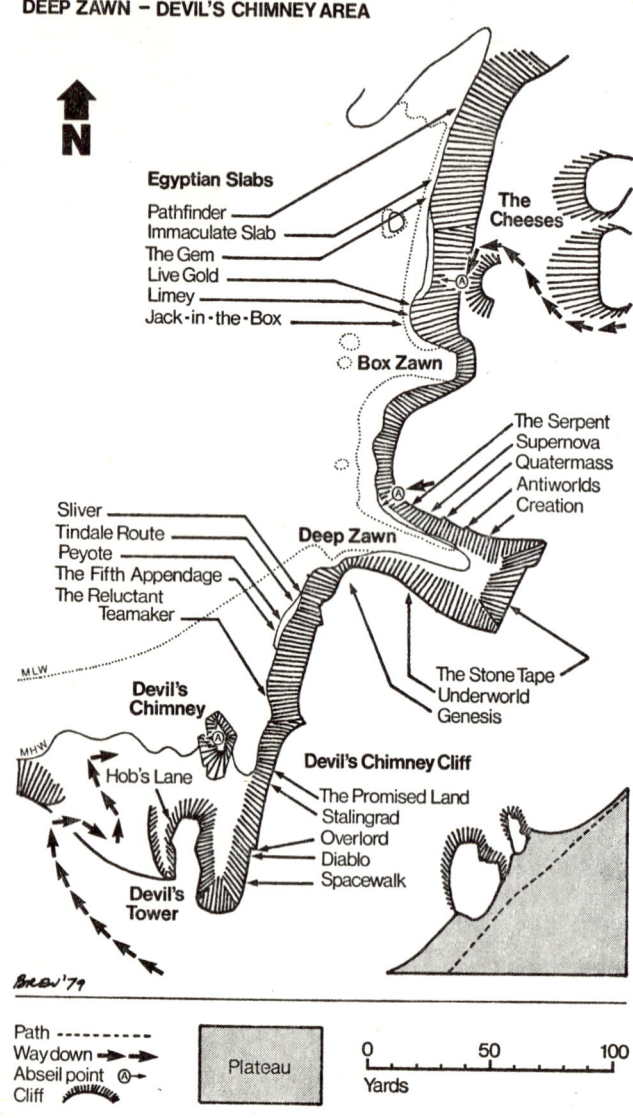

N

Egyptian Slabs
Pathfinder
Immaculate Slab
The Gem
Live Gold
Limey
Jack-in-the-Box

The Cheeses

Box Zawn

The Serpent
Supernova
Quatermass
Antiworlds
Creation

Sliver
Tindale Route
Peyote
The Fifth Appendage
The Reluctant
Teamaker

Deep Zawn

MLW

The Stone Tape
Underworld
Genesis

Devil's Chimney

MHW

Hob's Lane

Devil's Chimney Cliff
The Promised Land
Stalingrad
Overlord
Diablo
Spacewalk

Devil's Tower

BREW '79

Path - - - - - - -
Way down ➡
Abseil point Ⓐ➡
Cliff ⏜⏜⏜

Plateau

0   50   100
Yards

JENNY'S COVE

1 Limey
2 Live Gold
3 The Stone Tape
4 Underworld
5 Genesis
6 Sliver
7 Tindale Route
8 Peyote
9 Fifth Appendage
10 The Promised Land
11 Stalingrad
12 Overlord
13 Spacewalk
14 Diablo
15 Hob's Lane

A South end of Egyptian Slabs
B Box Zawn
C Deep Zawn
D Devil's Chimney
E Devil's Tower

First Ascents

(AL) indicates alternate leads.

1961 June   **Gannet Front**   J Logan, R Shaw (AL)
Previously referred to as the Original Route. The finish as described: R S Macnair, N J Allen, April 1974

1961 June   **The Constable**   J Logan, R Shaw

1961 June   **The Devil's Slide**   K M Lawder, J Logan
The Direct Finish: P H Biven, April 1971

1961 June   **Needle Rock**   K M Lawder, E C Pyatt

1961 June   **The Devil's Chimney**   R Shaw, J Logan
Pitch 2 as described: R J Tancred, R S Macnair, August 1969

1962 Aug   **Flying Buttress**   P H Biven, C Fishwick, A Goodwin

1963 Easter   **Bideford Ridge**   P H Biven, C Fishwick (AL)

1963 April 13   **Crusader**   P H Biven, C Fishwick (AL)

1963 April 15   **Devil's Spine**   V N Stevenson, P H Biven, C Fishwick, A Goodwin
Pitch 3 was climbed by a diversion into the gully on the right. Pitch 3 as described: R D Moulton, P Cannings, G J Gilbert, 18 April 1973

1963 April 15   **Albion**   P H Biven, V N Stevenson (AL), C Fishwick
The Direct Finish: P H Biven, April 1971

1964 Summer   **Flake Route**   M Steele, C Dyson

1964 Oct   **Horseman's Route**   J F McBratney, P Gwilliam

1965 May   **The Obverse Route**   A Swan, B Martindale

1965 May 5   **Puffin's Parade**   B Martindale, J F McBratney (AL)

1965 May 5   **Diamond Solitaire**   J F McBratney, B Martindale (AL)
Originally climbed with some aid in wet conditions but climbed free the following day by the same party

1965 May   **Tindale Route**   B Martindale, T Wright, J F McBratney

1966 June 3   **Ember Wall**   R B Quine, D W Limbert

1966 July 9   **Arrowhead**   P Wenham, R S D Smith (AL)

1966 Sept 28   **Seal Slab**   I M Peters, K M Lawder, M G White

1966 Sept 28   **Crenellation Groove**   I M Peters, K M Lawder

1967 Mar 26   **Saladin**   G Clarke, J B Cooper

1967 Mar 27   **The Squirmer**   G Clarke, J B Cooper

1967 Mar 28	**Dyke**	M J Luetchford, J Barraclough
1967 Mar 28	**Start**	J Barraclough, M J Luetchford
1967 Mar 29	**Integrity**	D W Brown, P Bingham, J Gill, J A Gaskill
1967 Mar 30	**Rehabilitation Wall**	J B Cooper (solo)
1967 Mar 30	**Norseman**	M J Luetchford, J Barraclough
1967 Mar 30	**Forgotten Pinnacle**	J Barraclough, M J Luetchford
1967 Mar 31	**Stingray**	J Barraclough, M J Luetchford
1967 Mar 31	**Cornflake Crack**	G Clarke, M J Luetchford
1967 June	**Walrus**	S Dawson, D Rogers (AL)
1968 May	**Fag Ash**	W N Tolfree, K Vickery
1968 May	**Alice**	K Vickery, D Vickery
1968 Sept	**White Horse**	R J Ebdon, H A M Warren
1969 April 28	**Long Ruse Ridge**	K M Lawder, I M Peters (AL), M E B Banks

The variations were climbed by S Westmacott and M Westmacott in September 1975 as Long Ruse Ridge Direct, and by I Richards, P Rogers in August 1979 as a climb called Goat

1969 May 14	**Twelve Bore**	G Raymont, S Miller
1969 May 23	**Force Eight**	W N Tolfree, G Raymont
1969 May 23	**Stuka**	G Raymont, W N Tolfree
1969 July 20	**Short Story**	S Miller, K Vickery
1969 Aug	**Punchbowl Arête**	R D Moulton, J L Moulton
1969 Sept 26	**Transition**	M E B Banks, K M Lawder, J Douglas
1969 Sept 30	**Cable Way**	I M Peters, M E B Banks (AL)
1970 Mar 29	**Satan's Slip**	L P Fatti, D G Ward
1970 Mar 29	**Dexter**	T J Kerrich, L P Fatti

Climbed in reverse as a climb finishing up Devil's Spine. Climbed as an approach to Fluted Face by R D Moulton, T D Thompson, 8 May 1971

1970 Mar 31	**Focal Face**	T J Kerrich, L P Fatti (AL)
1970 Aug 1	**The Bow**	L P Fatti, T J Kerrich
1970 Aug 29	**Devil Dodger**	R D Moulton, R B Stone (AL)
1970 Aug 29	**Forget-me-Not**	J Hammond, R D Moulton
1970 Aug 29	**The Kiln**	I F Howell, P H Biven (AL)
1970 Aug 29	**Ulysses Factor**	P H Biven, I F Howell (AL)
1970 Aug 30	**Cable and Wireless**	P H Biven, I F Howell (AL)
1970 Sept 25	**Big Shiner**	W F Wright, V N Bentinck
1971 April 8	**Pony and Trap**	P H Biven, B M Biven, A Alvarez
1971 April 8	**Lucifer**	P H Biven, A Alvarez
1971 May 7	**Ramrod**	P R Littlejohn, M C Chambers
1971 May 8	**Albacore**	P R Littlejohn, M C Chambers
1971 May 9	**Magnificat**	F E R Cannings, K J Wilson
1971 May 9	**Juggernaut**	P R Littlejohn, M C Chambers

1971 May 10   **Performance**   F E R Cannings, K J Wilson
Pitch 1 was climbed as a climb called Sinister by
L P Fatti, T J Kerrich, 29 March 1970
1971 July 6   **The Summons**   K Darbyshire, P H Biven
1971 July 6   **Eveninawl**   J Cleare, K Darbyshire, P H Biven
1971 July 8   **Shark**   K Darbyshire, P H Biven
1971 Aug 22   **St Peter's Stone**   F E R Cannings (solo)
1971 Aug 23   **Blood Axe**   O Eliasson, P H Biven, J Cleare
1971 Aug 23   **Siegfried**   P H Biven, A Chadwick
1971 Aug 23   **Seventh Seal**   K J Wilson, P W Thexton
1971 Aug 25   **Sundance**   R D Moulton, K J Wilson
1971 Aug 26   **Valhalla**   P W Thexton, C J Henwood
1971 Aug 27   **Hel**   P W Thexton, C J Henwood
Climbed with one point of aid
1971 Sept 24   **Quadratus Lumborum**   C J Lawrence, J Brown,
S D Perry, A D Caswell
1971 Sept 24   **Talcum**   G W H Smith, I Marriott
1971 Sept 25   **Hurricane**   C J Lawrance, J Brown, A D Caswell,
I Marriott
1972 Mar 17   **Shamrock**   T D Thompson, R D Moulton (AL),
P B deMengel
The fall of a large flake completely changed the
character of the top pitch—this was re-climbed in
September 1977 by W Parker and is now the Direct
Finish. The present second pitch was climbed in
October 1974 by K Darbyshire, S B Jones and the
top pitch was the original finish to Evictor
1972 Mar 19   **Alpine Ridge**   R D Moulton, T D Thompson (AL)
1972 Mar 19   **Garden Rake**   T D Thompson, R D Moulton (AL)
1972 Mar 19   **Occidental Groove**   R D Moulton, T D Thompson
(AL)
1972 Mar 19   **Zig Zag Zig**   S D Roberts, W F Wright (AL)
On Second Buttress North, now destroyed
1972 Mar 20   **Scafoid**   P B deMengel, K Roche
Climbed with one point of aid. The variation, Foot
Off, was climbed in April 1972 by G Rigby, N
Stuart
1972 Mar 29   **Time Bomb**   P R Littlejohn, C A G Morton
With two points of aid. Climbed free by P R
Littlejohn in August 1977
1972 Mar 31   **The Black Hand**   K Darbyshire, I F Duckworth,
A McFarlane
1972 Mar 31   **The Stray**   P R Littlejohn, C A G Morton

1972 April 1   **Evictor**   P R Littlejohn, K Darbyshire
The original finish has now been used for Shamrock.
The present finish was first climbed in October 1974
by K Darbyshire, S B Jones as part of an
exploratory route called Ringroad

1972 April 2   **The Minstrel**   C A G Morton, P R Littlejohn (AL)
On Second Buttress North, now destroyed

1972 April 2   **Scrabble**   I F Duckworth, A D McFarlane

1972 April 2   **Destiny**   P R Littlejohn, C A G Morton

1972 April 3   **Cow Pie**   K Darbyshire, C A G Morton

1972 April 3   **Rampart**   P R Littlejohn, A McFarlane, I F
Duckworth

1972 May 30   **Centaur**   C J Lawrance, A D Caswell
With one point of aid on the top pitch, in an
ungardened state. Cleaned and climbed free by P R
Littlejohn in September 1972

1972 Sept 6   **Formula One**   P R Littlejohn, R D Moulton,
G J Gilbert

1972 Sept 7   **Motorman**   G J Gilbert, R D Moulton

1972 Sept 9   **Road Runner**   G J Gilbert, P R Littlejohn, R D
Moulton

1972 Sept 10   **Overlord**   G J Gilbert, R D Moulton, P R
Littlejohn

1972 Sept 10   **Wodwo**   P R Littlejohn, R D Moulton

1972 Sept 11   **Antiworlds**   P R Littlejohn, R D Moulton

1973 April 15   **Dihedral**   P R Littlejohn, C A G Morton

1973 April 15   **Flashback**   F E R Cannings, J W A Kingston (AL)

1973 April 16   **Quatermass**   K Darbyshire, H Clarke
Climbed with a number of points of aid.
Subsequently climbed with one point of aid by P R
Littlejohn in April 1973 and free by R Evans in
October 1974

1973 April 16   **The Serpent**   P R Littlejohn, C A G Morton (AL)

1973 April 16   **Beamsplitter**   J W A Kingston, F E R Cannings
(AL)

1973 April 16   **Jetset**   F E R Cannings, J W A Kingston
With two aid points for resting. Climbed free by
P R Littlejohn in 1977

1973 April 17   **The Stone Tape**   P R Littlejohn, K Darbyshire
With 3 pegs for aid and the tension traverse.
Climbed entirely free in (the unusually dry conditions
of) 1976 by R Harrison

1973 April 17   **The Reluctant Teamaker**   I F Duckworth, A
McFarlane (AL)

1973 April 17 **Bender** F E R Cannings, J W A Kingston
With two aid points for resting. Climbed free by P R Littlejohn in 1977

1973 April 17 **Quandary** F E R Cannings, J W A Kingston (AL), P Cannings

1973 April 17 **Sandpiper** G J Gilbert, R D Moulton

1973 April 17 **Magic Flute** R D Moulton, G J Gilbert

1973 April 17 **Good Vibrations** G J Gilbert, R D Moulton

1973 April 18 **Frontispiece** F E R Cannings, J W A Kingston (AL), P Cannings

1973 April 18 **The Arch** J W A Kingston and F E R Cannings (solo)

1973 April 18 **The Fifth Appendage** A McFarlane, I F Duckworth (AL)

1973 April 18 **Navigator** P R Littlejohn, C A G Morton

1973 April 18 **Footnote** F E R Cannings, J W A Kingston (AL)

1973 April 19 **Digitalis** G J Gilbert, R D Moulton

1973 April 19 **Purple People Eater** J W A Kingston, F E R Cannings

1973 April 19 **Headline** F E R Cannings, J W A Kingston (AL)

1973 April 19 **Sambo** K Darbyshire, H Clarke
Variation: P R Littlejohn, K Darbyshire, 12 April 1974

1973 April 19 **Chair Ladder** K Darbyshire, H Clarke

1973 April 19 **Creation** P R Littlejohn, C A G Morton (AL)

1973 April 20 **Epicentre** K Darbyshire (solo)

1973 April 20 **Supernova** P R Littlejohn, C A G Morton

1973 April 20 **Tempest** G J Gilbert, R D Moulton (AL)

1973 April 20 **Papa Joe** F E R Cannings, J W A Kingston, P Cannings

1973 April 20 **Margin** F E R Cannings, J W A Kingston

1973 April 21 **Prospero** G J Gilbert, R D Moulton

1973 April 21 **Stop Press** F E R Cannings, J W Kingston (AL)

1973 April 21 **Rainbow** J W A Kingston, F E R Cannings

1973 April 21 **Underworld** P R Littlejohn, K Darbyshire (AL)

1973 July 7 **Atlantic Reject** P H Biven, C P Gibson, J D Fowler

1973 July 7 **Celtic Shield** J D Fowler, C P Gibson, J Pike

1973 July 21 **Hunky Dory** J Lister, M Putnam

1973 July 23 **Moby Dick** J Lister, M Putnam

1973 Sept 5 **Breakaway** P W Thexton, P Whitear

1973 Sept 6 **Bloody Ages** P Whitear, P W Thexton

1973 Sept 7 **Flak** P W Thexton, P Whitear

1973 Sept 7 **Tracer** P W Thexton, P Whitear

1973 Sept 25	**Vallum**	R J F Brown, C J Lawrance (AL)

Alternative Finish: A J Parker, G Thomas, 23 April 1975

1973 Oct 4   **The Green Light**   P W Thexton, R Owen, R G Cooper

1973 Oct 5   **The Vice**   P W Thexton, R G Cooper

1973 Oct 6   **Arch Fiend**   P W Thexton, R G Cooper

1973 Oct 6   **The Flue**   P W Thexton, R G Cooper

1974 Mar 20   **Irish Roulette**   C P Gibson, N Stein

1974 Mar 25   **Strider**   C P Gibson, N Stein, R Dorkins, S P Braim

1974 April 12   **Peyote**   A McFarlane, D Hardy

1974 April 13   **Echo**   J de Montjoye, J Brennen, T Walker, D Irons

1974 April 13   **Diablo**   P R Littlejohn, K Darbyshire (AL)

1974 April 13   **Wolfman Jack**   P W Thexton, K J Wilson

With four points of aid. This was reduced to two by P W Thexton in April 1974 and again by P R Littlejohn to one point in 1977. Climbed free by R Edwards in August 1979. American Graffiti Finish: K Wilkinson, G Hounson, August 1978

1974 April 14   **Blue Jaunt**   P R Littlejohn, K Darbyshire

1974 April 14   **Stalingrad**   P R Littlejohn, K J Wilson

1974 April 14   **Round the Horn**   K Darbyshire (solo)

1974 April 15   **Immaculate Slab**   P W Thexton, K J Wilson

1974 April 15   **Pathfinder**   P W Thexton, R D Moulton

With one peg for aid, which was eliminated by P W Thexton in April 1974

1974 April 16   **The Promised Land**   P R Littlejohn, K Darbyshire

1974 April 16   **Wild Country**   P R Littlejohn, K Darbyshire

1974 April 16   **The Gem**   P W Thexton, R D Moulton

1974 April 17   **Hob's Lane**   K Darbyshire, P R Littlejohn

1974 April 17   **The Mexican Connection**   A McFarlane, K J Wilson (AL)

1974 April 18   **Spacewalk**   P R Littlejohn, K Darbyshire (AL), P W Thexton

1974 April 25   **Live Gold**   P W Thexton, N Groves

1974 April 25   **Limey**   P W Thexton, N Groves

1974 April 26   **Conger**   P W Thexton, N Groves

1974 Sept 19   **Jug of Punch**   R Hughes, D McGowan

1974 Oct   **Montague Python**   K Darbyshire, S B Jones

1974 Oct 16   **The Good Ship Lollipop**   C Phillips, M Barnicott (AL)

1974 Oct 16   **Hooka**   C Phillips, M Barnicott (AL)

1974 Oct 16   **Sunblest**   C Phillips, M Barnicott (AL)

1974 Oct 16	**The Queen's Gambit** R Evans, M Sharp, P W Thexton

1974 Oct 16 **The Queen's Gambit** R Evans, M Sharp, P W
Thexton
1975 Mar 27 **Way Out** L R Holliwell, E Brook
1975 Mar 28 **Blizzard** L R Holliwell, E Brook
1975 Mar 29 **Jack-in-the-Box** M Putnam, J Lister
1975 Mar 31 **Messin' with the Kid** P R Littlejohn, D C Garner
1975 Mar 31 **American Beauty** P R Littlejohn, D C Garner
1975 April 3 **Verdict** P R Littlejohn, D C Garner
1975 April 3 **Apsara** N J Allen, R D Moulton
1975 July **Umbgozi** R Ballie, J Cunningham
1975 Sept **Slab and Groove** S Read
1975 Sept **Salty Slip** S Read
*Climbed as a variation start to Slab and Groove,
named from an ascent in 1979 by B Goodwin, J Vose*
1976 April 18 **Eclipse** F E R Cannings, A Strapcans (AL), S
Berry
*By the Right Hand Start. The ordinary start was
climbed by F E R Cannings in August 1977*
1976 April 18 **Winkle Picker** A Strapcans, F E R Cannings, S
Berry
1976 April 19 **Mirage Oasis** A Strapcans, F E R Cannings (AL)
1976 April 21 **Saturday Night** S Berry, P Cannings
1976 April 21 **Sunday Morning** S Berry, P Cannings
1976 April 23 **Labyrinth** F E R Cannings, A Strapcans (AL)
1976 April 24 **The Exorcist** A Strapcans, F E R Cannings (AL)
1976 April 26 **Biggles** A Strapcans and F E R Cannings (solo)
1976 Aug 30 **Sexcrime** A Strapcans, F E R Cannings
1976 Aug 31 **Bleed for Speed** A Strapcans, F E R Cannings
1976 Sept 3 **Pinstripe** C Wand-Tetley, W Hoy, B Scott
1976 Sept 20 **Devil's Honeymoon** D Langmead, R McElligott
1977 April 8 **Muffin the Mule** F E R Cannings, A Strapcans
1977 April 9 **Gulf Stream** F E R Cannings, A Strapcans
1977 April 10 **Fusion** F E R Cannings, A Strapcans
1977 April 11 **Hot Rod** C Wand-Tetley, J G Phillips
1977 April 11 **Scorched Earth** A Strapcans, F E R Cannings
1977 April 11 **Lemon Pie** D Tempest, M Newton
1977 April 14 **The Great Divide** F E R Cannings, A Strapcans
*Climbed with a total of five points of aid (two for
resting). This was reduced to three by P R Littlejohn
in August 1977*
1977 July **Escape Route** S Lees, P Horth (AL), R. Wainer,
M Willbourn
1977 Aug 4 **Flashing into the Dark** T Jones, R Hughes
1977 Aug 22 **Astral Traveller** P R Littlejohn, C King, F E R
Cannings

1977 Aug 23	**Beam Up** P R Littlejohn, F E R Cannings
1977 Aug 26	**Captain Cat** F E R Cannings, P R Littlejohn (AL)
1977 Aug 27	**Golden Gate** P R Littlejohn F E R Cannings
1977 Aug 27	**The Minatour** C King, C K Wand-Tetley
1977 Aug 28	**Olympica** P R Littlejohn, C King
1977 Aug 28	**Conga Corner** R J Berry, C K Wand-Tetley
1977 Aug 28	**Funky Chicken** C K Wand-Tetley, R J Berry
1977 Aug 28	**Pancake Shuffle** R J Berry, C K Wand-Tetley (AL)
1978 Aug 2	**Dark Power** R J Hughes, L McGinley
1978 Aug 3	**Redspeed** R J Hughes, L McGinley
1978 Aug	**Genesis** K Wilkinson, G Hounson
1978 Sept 1	**Sliver** B R E Wilkinson, A Gallagher
1978 Oct 5	**The Lantern Man** R Dean, K Lyle (AL)
1978 Oct 9	**Lady in White** K Lyle, R Dean (AL)
1978 Oct 22	**Big Ed** P G James, E J Kamp
1978 Oct 24	**Diamond Crack** P G James, T W McDonald
1979 April 20	**Jude the Obscure** B R E Wilkinson, A Gallagher
1979 April 26	**Reprise** B R E Wilkinson, A Gallagher
1979 April 26	**Salty Dog** B R E Wilkinson, A Gallagher
1979 Aug 8	**Starship Trooper** M Hunt, M Elms, V Ho
1979 Aug 8	**Solomon Grundy** M Hunt, M Elms, V Ho
1979 Aug 9	**Channel Wrack** B Goodwin, J Vose
1979 Aug 10	**St Loosifer** M Hunt, V Ho
1979 Aug	**Out of the Blue** B Goodwin, J Vose
1979 Aug 11	**A Separate Reality** D Carr, T Cowcill
1979 Aug 11	**Gorgeous Guano** M Cox, B Goodwin, J Vose, P Thompson
1979 Aug 27	**Illusion** A Gallagher, C Nicholson
1979 Aug 28	**Demian** B R E Wilkinson, S R Bondi
1979 Aug 29	**Incantations** A Stewart, P Liptrot (AL)
1979 Aug 29	**Rusty Silk** C Nicholson, A Gallagher
1979 Aug 30	**Grand Falls Road** R Edwards, S Salmon
1979 Aug 31	**Pomplemouse** C Nicholson, B R E Wilkinson
1979 Aug 31	**The China Syndrome** R Edwards, S Salmon
1979 Aug 31	**Streaky** S A Lewis, A Stewart *The first pitch was added by R Guest, G Robinson on* 15 *September* 1979
1979 Aug 31	**Fifty Pumps** P Scraton, A Stewart (AL)
1979 Sept 1	**White Riot** R P Hastings, M Winstanley
1979 Sept 17	**Spanner** F A S Robinson, F Lunnan

Index

Rescue

Lundy is designated as a sub-post by the Mountain Rescue Committee. A Thomas stretcher, First Aid kit and two 320-foot manila ropes for stretcher-hauling are kept on the island. N.B. At the time of writing, the rope was as provided in 1972 and therefore its condition should be subject to scrutiny.

In the event of an accident, report immediately to the Administrator's office, or to his house when the office is shut. Give the exact location of the accident but avoid using climbers' names for cliffs which are not common usage on the island— Arch Zawn, Torrey Canyon, Weird Wall etc. (i.e. features not marked on the map in the Lundy handbook or on the map sold in the shop) mean nothing to non-climbers. If, on the West Coast, there is any possible doubt as to the description of the location leave a prominent marker (such as clothing, rucsacs etc.) on the coastal path.

If necessary, the island authorities will make a request for an Air/Sea Rescue helicopter and the possibility of having the casualty winched direct into a helicopter should be taken into account. It should also be borne in mind that the Thomas stretcher is too large to be carried inside some helicopters— normally the helicopter's stretcher should be available. An alternative possibility is for the casualty to be evacuated by boat but this depends on the location, the sea and on a boat being available.

If a stretcher-haul has to be made, manpower is essential. Due to the nature of the terrain, it can be difficult to find safe anchorage points at the top of the cliff and there is often a considerable risk of boulders being dislodged by the haul ropes. If the climbing party is large enough, it is advisable for one climber to stay at plateau level to liaise with the islanders. Morphia is kept with the First Aid kit and is also kept by the keeper of the North Light. It must be remembered that the islanders, whilst very resourceful and capable, are not climbers. Therefore, they can not be expected to understand climbing terminology or to take climbing risks.

After an accident a written report should be sent to the Hon. Secretary, Mountain Rescue Committee, 9 Milldale Avenue, Temple Mears, Buxton, Derbyshire, giving details of: date of accident, extent of injuries, name, age and address of casualty, and MRC equipment used.